# Broadcast Engineering and IT Conference 2021



Online
9-13 October 2021

ISBN: 978-1-7138-3933-0

**Printed from e-media with permission by:**

Curran Associates, Inc.
57 Morehouse Lane
Red Hook, NY 12571

Some format issues inherent in the e-media version may also appear in this print version.



National Association of Broadcasters (NAB)
1 M Street SE
Washington, D.C. 20003

Phone: (202) 429 5300

www.nab.org

**Additional copies of this publication are available from:**

Curran Associates, Inc.
57 Morehouse Lane
Red Hook, NY 12571 USA
Phone: 845-758-0400
Fax: 845-758-2633
Email: curran@proceedings.com
Web: www.proceedings.com

# TABLE OF CONTENTS

## AI AND CLOUD TECHNOLOGIES FOR BROADCASTING



## MITIGATING FACILITY RISKS - CYBER & PHYSICAL



## SMPTE ST2110 - IP-BASED FACILITIES

# Cloud Live Production: The New Resource Perspectives for Media Tech Broadcasters – A Case Study

**Carlos Cesar Abrahão**
**Globo**
**Rio de Janeiro, Rio de Janeiro, Brazil**
carlos.abrahao@g.globo

**Abstract** –In this case study we will address the premises, choice of protocols, technologies, analysis of challenges and the development of a system on public cloud that allow the production of live content for transmission to over-the air (OTA), Pay TV, over-the-top TV (OTT), Social Media streaming and other platforms. This system is alive and must be resilient to new technologies to guarantee future-proofing of the system, accepting the exchange or updating of one or more modules up to just prior to airtime.

## Introduction

Globo's production content covers more than 200 daily hours, among more than 10 television channels. Regarding sports content, it is covered about 3500 events per year, delivered among all platforms. Globo's OTT platform has UHD content as well produced by Itself, such as recorded live shows, tv series and soap operas. The on-premises infrastructure is mainly HD format, among SDI and SDI-IP standards like ST292, ST2022-6 and ST2110, with more than 20 studios and control rooms. Regarding the OTA, the company has 5 main sites in different regions of the country and delivers its content to almost 120 affiliates.

Due to this large amount of content productions, Globo needs a flexible, scalable and dynamic infrastructure. The traditional and solid on-premises systems are considered static, since the number of productions is limited to the amount of equipment that you have in-house. In the other hand, it is reasonable to have an infrastructure able to achieve the audio and video quality compatible to the business and delivery, like OTA, OTT, Pay TV and streaming service platforms. That was the opportunity to study and evaluate the use of cloud environments in order to produce live entertainment, journalism and sports content.

A traditional way of producing live content is shown in Figure 1.

This paper is excerpted from the Proceedings of the 2021 NAB Broadcast Engineering and Information Technology (BEIT) Conference, © 2021, National Association of Broadcasters, 1 M Street S.E., Washington, DC 20003 USA.

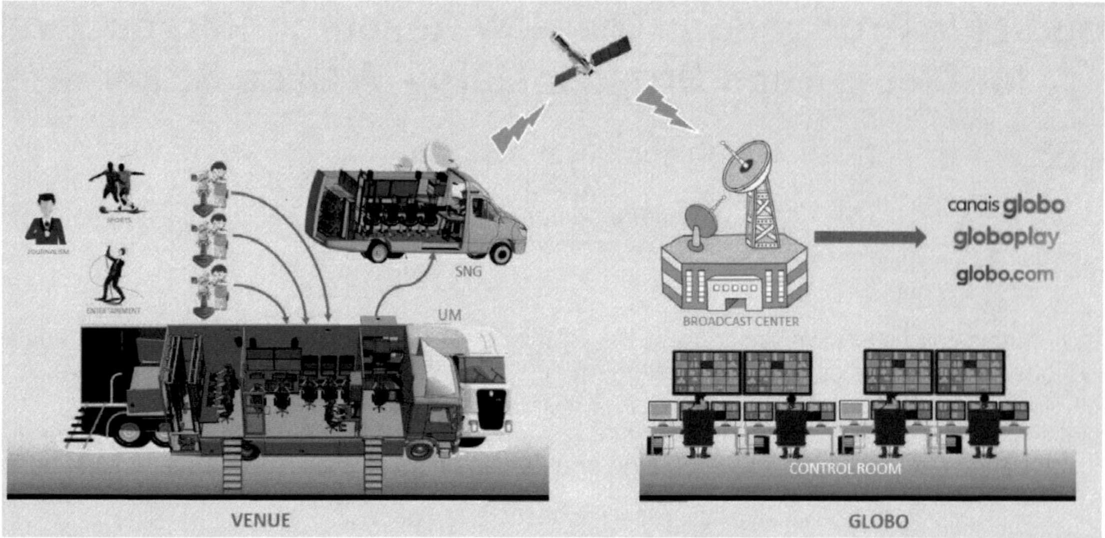


FIGURE 1: TRADITIONAL CONTENT-PRODUCTION PATH

The productions usually have a remote production vehicle and portable satellite uplink at the venue able to produce the live signals, providing audio and video mixing, instant replays and graphics related to the events, like scores, stats and lower thirds. At the on-premises control room, some content enrichments are added into the event, such as clip playouts from other events during the interval time, live signals from parallel programs, in-house studio camera feeds and extra graphics and lower thirds. Some similar resources are provided to screens at the venue, improving the experience for the live audience, as well.

So, there is an opportunity to merge all these resources into a cloud environment that will manage both productions, at the venue and for the broadcast, as Figure 2 illustrates.

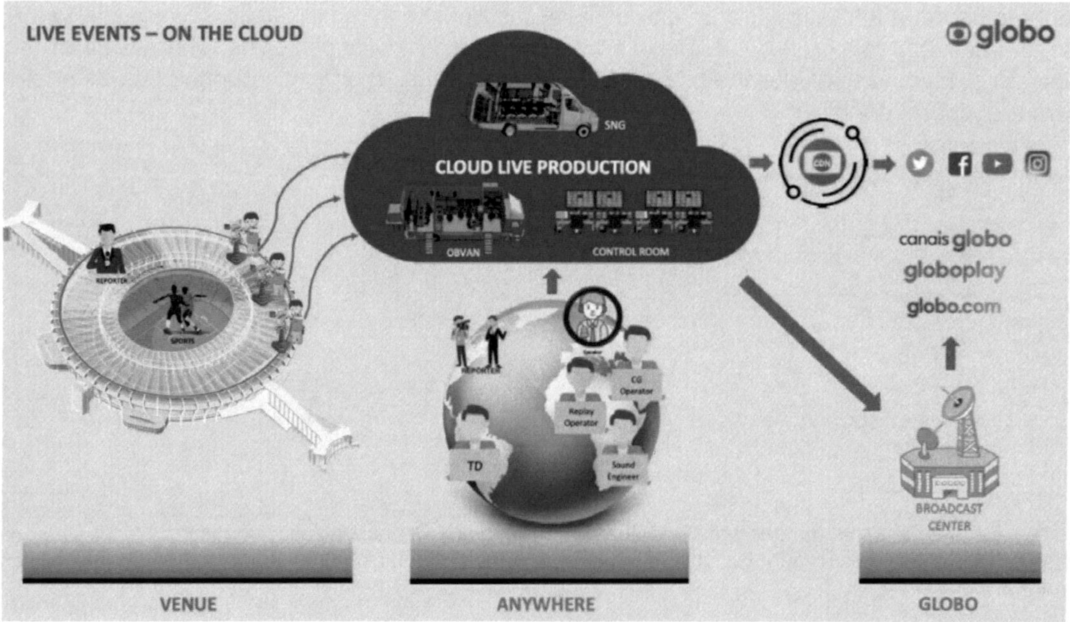


FIGURE 2: MERGING THE RESOURCES OF VENUE AND BROADCAST CONTROL ROOM

It is important to mention that this new scenario provides the sharing of all events' resources anywhere, allowing the crew to be physically located in different parts of the world. The cloud environment developed by Globo team involved large-scale integration among many vendors in the market. Since a single solution covering all resources necessary for live production was not found, we co-developed a solution required for events' workflow, and we studied the best practices among the broadcast and internet ecosystems, such as latency issues for the signal flows and remote access for operators.

## High Level Architecture

A new solution architecture was designed according to the concept shown in Figure 3. These were the project guidelines:

- **Venue and Host Contributions:** Audio, video, operational control and tally must be sent in a secure way, with reliability to the cloud platform.
- **Cloud Services:** Video Switcher, Audio Mixer, Clip Player, Instant Replay, CG, AV Processing, Encoding, Intercom must be on a cloud platform, and their signals interoperable from vendors.
- **Intercom server on cloud:** Clients on workstations and mobile devices, connection to on-premises systems, with ability to conference or set up individual communication channels.
- **Fast Contributions:** Talent and guests must be able to be connected to the cloud from anywhere, via webcams and mobile devices.
- **Product Asset Management (PAM) and Media Asset Management (MAM) integration with the cloud platform:** Must provide a seamless experience to the viewer.
- **Operator's crew:** Can operate the platform from anywhere via public internet.
- **Delivery:** On-premises broadcast facilities and Content Distribution Network (CDN).

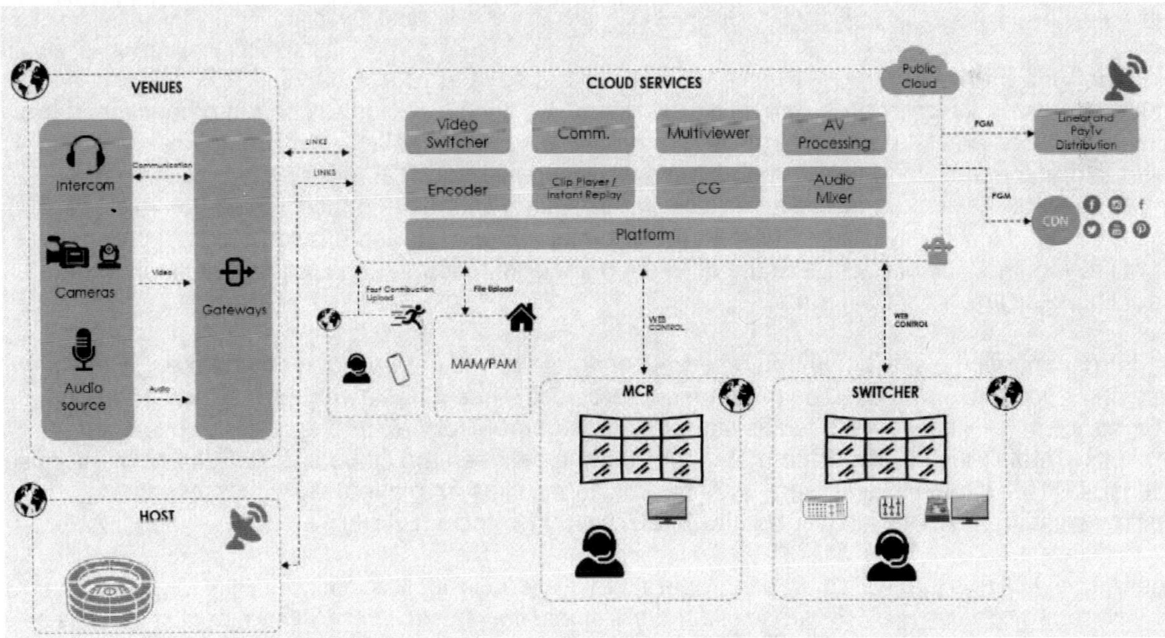


FIGURE 3: HIGH-LEVEL ARCHITECTURE

## Implementing Solutions in a Cloud Environment

Globo is producing its events in Google Cloud Platform (GCP) using the architecture as shown in Figure 4.

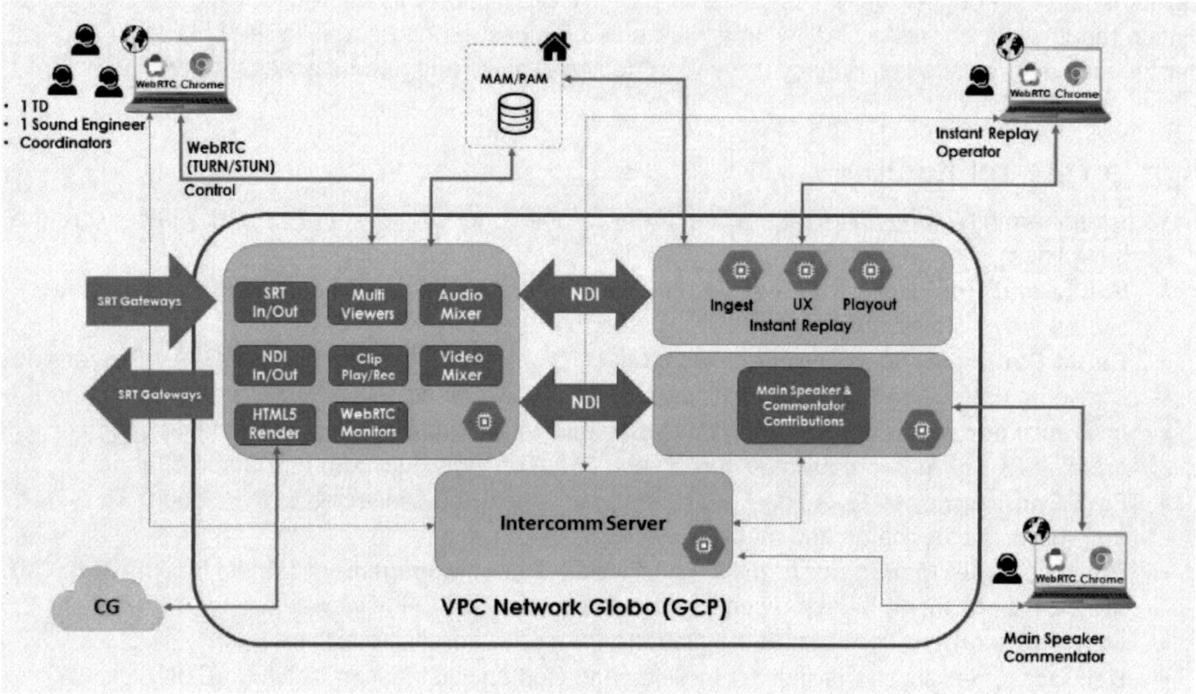


FIGURE 4: GLOBO'S CURRENT CLOUD ENVIRONMENT

Inside the Virtual Private Cloud (VPC) network, there are several virtual machine (VM) instances in infrastructure as a service (IaaS), providing the resources necessary to the content production in the event. When located at the same instance, the resource applications act as microservices, and it is desirable that the audio and video signals have uncompressed or near lossless formats, like the formats available in on-premises systems. An important advantage of platform based on microservices is the ability to dynamically create, delete, start and stop resources, and provide “tiers” of productions that will fit with the type of event, like the different number of resources that can be found in remote production vehicles or control rooms.

In order to connect the signals among different vendor solutions on the cloud environment, Network Digital Interface (NDI) was used as the transport protocol, since it has a very low latency and good performance in LAN networks, besides being an interoperable format among many solutions on the market. Regarding the pre-recorded material exchange between the cloud and PAM/MAM on-premises systems, MXF XDCAM HD files were used to provide the clips for playout during the event, in a workflow sending the material over Secure File-Transfer Protocol (SFTP).

Regarding the clients that will control and operate the resource applications, the user experience (UX) views were provided as HTTPS web links, and the signal flows used WebRTC protocol, since it is a very low latency format compatible with the monitoring resources for the crew, like multiviewers and program / preset views.

As an option, guest contributions could be connected to the cloud ecosystem by WebRTC connections, as well. It was chosen to reduce the latency to this connection and to be simple to the user connecting by a computer or a mobile device.

We used an open-source, cloud-based intercom solution, where each operator having a client application was logically allocated in a sub-channel of a channel on system. These channels or subchannels work as a conference, where all members talk among them. There is also the possibility of a private communication between operators. The intercom user interface was handled with keyboard shortcuts from the same workstation that runs the other applications related to the event, like instant replay and video mixer control, minimizing the number of devices necessary for the operation.

## Transmission from Venues to the Cloud

The setup validated to connect the Venue and Cloud is illustrated in Figure 5.

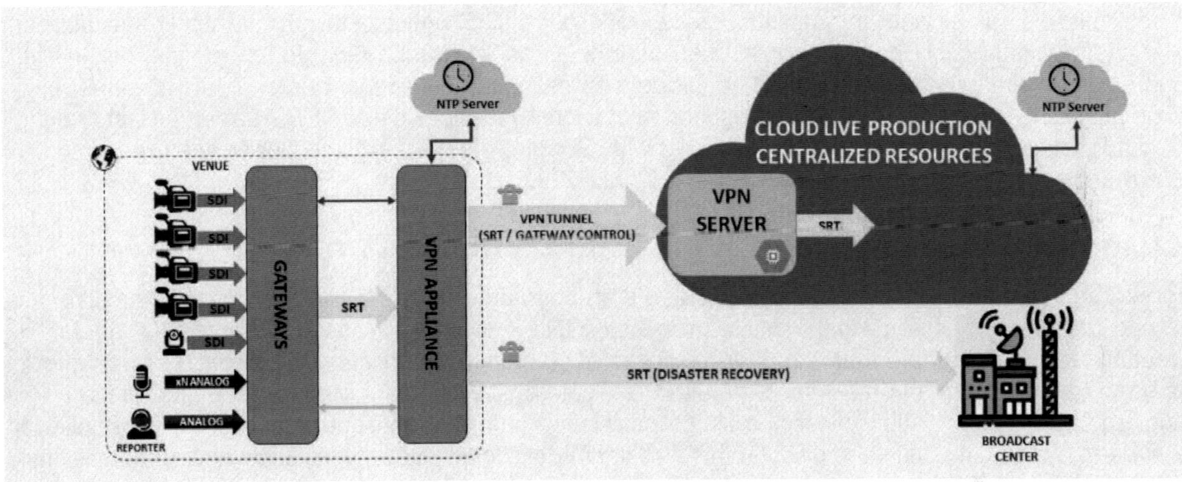


FIGURE 5: WORKFLOW AT VENUE

The open-source transport protocol chosen to carry all audio and video signals from the venue was Secure Reliable Transport (SRT), due to its security (AES128 / AES256 encryption), resilience and reliability through the internet. The transported video and audio compression streams were H.264 / H.265, up to 15Mbps, and MPEG4 LC-AAC 2/0 @ 192kbps, respectively. Other formats, like OPUS (another good choice for compression of ambience and voice audio), were also trialed.

A Virtual Private Network (VPN) appliance provided a tunnel for the SRT feeds, giving and additional protection layer against internet piracy, and simplifying the connection procedure between the gateways and resource applications responsible for receiving SRT feeds in the cloud.

To provide a contingency plan in case of a cloud failure, we sent a secondary SRT stream carrying the main camera video signal embedded with several microphones to maintain live content from the venue while the cloud environment was reestablished.

An important topic regarding video encoding at the venue is time alignment. In order to have all signals presented without any timing difference among them, both sides (venue and video processing applications on cloud environment) must be synchronized with the same time basis. We chose Network Time Protocol (NTP) for this purpose. In H.264 and H.265 video codecs, we used Supplemental Enhanced Information (SEI) metadata, which can send picture timestamps for every video frame, in hh:mm:ss:ff clock format. Enabling this feature on video encoders into the gateways, the video processing applications on cloud side calculates the timing difference among the coming feeds and increase buffers to have all signals being processed at same time on video mixer, giving the same result as found in on-premises equipment.

## Transmission from Cloud to Delivery

SRT transport protocol was chosen to carry the program feed from cloud to the broadcast center as well, where similar gateways as those on the venue side were used, in order to convert the signals to HD-SDI, ST2022-6 or ST2110 at on-premises facilities, following the same paths once used by traditional control-room program feeds.

Real Time Messaging Protocol (RTMP) was chosen to send the same program signal from the cloud directly to CDN infrastructure available in Globo's OTT platforms due to the legacy and Social Media compatibility.

Cloud providers can extend an on-premises network to the VPC network through a highly available and lower latency connection than the public internet. In this case, we used Google Interconnect from the cloud environment in São Paulo, Brazil, to Globo's on-premises broadcast center in Rio de Janeiro, Brazil, providing round-trip time (RTT) results lower than 10 msec. Besides SRT streams (first used with public internet), future tests are scheduled with Google Interconnect in order to see the performance of other protocols, like NDI and ST2022-2.

## Automation, Scheduling and Monitoring Cloud Resources

Beyond the benefits of using this flexible, scalable and dynamic structure on the cloud, it was also deemed necessary to automate the whole process so that it could be properly managed by regular operating teams. To enable that, the entire process of planning and creating the structure of an event has been mapped, and an on-demand, self-service, catalog-based planning interface has been designed to bring automation to every task. Once relevant information about the event was supplied to the system by the user interface portal (start and finish date/time, event type, assigned personnel and their roles), an automation process in the backend software was created based on the information, and the system ran at the date/time planned for the event, providing the availability of the necessary structure so it was ready to be used as previously scheduled. The diagram related to this automated process is shown in Figure 6.

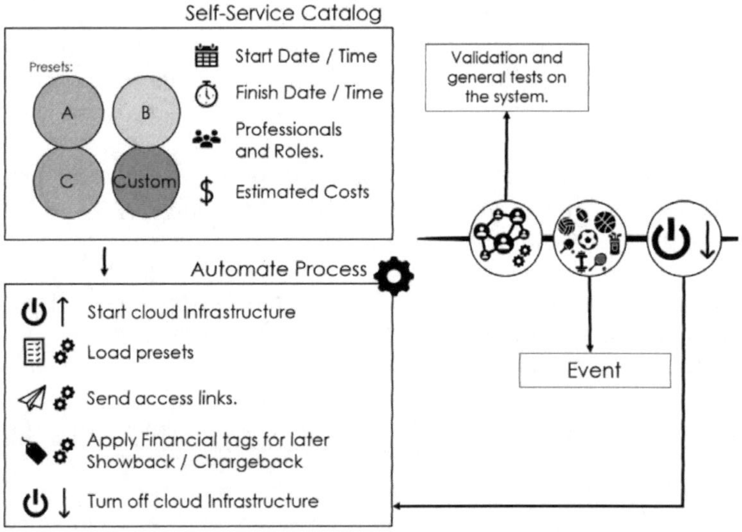


FIGURE 6: SCHEDULED AUTOMATION FOR EVENT

To guarantee that the system is working properly while the event is running, some monitoring dashboards must be supplied for the technical operational teams in charge of it. That is a critical point because many solutions degrade performance and reliability at specific levels of infrastructure and/or network resource consumption, and they might compromise the show.

Items like CPU, memory, networking, health of the streaming and components are continuously monitored and displayed. Alerts and alarms are also set to call the attention of the technical team in case of any needs of adjustment or intervention. Figure 7 shows one such monitoring dashboard.

FIGURE 7: EXAMPLE OF INFRASTRUCTURE MONITORING DASHBOARD

## Conclusion

In the transformation of a content-production and broadcasting company to a media technology organization, it is necessary to go beyond the quality and reliability that have already been achieved and incorporate innovative concepts. These required innovations will enable the efficiency, elasticity and flexibility needed to increase content production and distribution volume, with agility to deliver the content via all available pipes, all while deploying technical and human resources to distributed locations under centralized management.

This revised architecture provides an easily scalable way to meet the needs of new business opportunities. It is also resilient to obstacles imposed by environmental and social challenges, cataclysmic events, pandemics, and other difficulties.

The ability to have talent and technical teams working together in different locations overcomes the physical or temporal barriers to production and delivery of live content worldwide. In order to manage this new platform, technology teams must implement best practices from both broadcast and IT industries, creating new knowledge and skill sets.

This case study shows the design and implementation of a new content-production platform architecture that is able to match the needs of the traditional broadcasting market, streaming services and other media delivery. This effort requires cooperative development with vendors such as broadcast, media-solution and cloud providers, and the harmonization of in-house solutions with open-source systems, thereby creating an elastic platform that can be modeled to increase the number of productions and avoid the spending of unnecessary resources.

This approach brings efficiency, flexibility and versatility that enables continuing evolution, providing adaptive and optimized solutions as each new business case is encountered.

# ColorNet 1.5: Improving Machine Learning Color Correction for Video

**Michelle Mayer, Erica B. Walker, D. Hudson Smith**
**Clemson University**
**Clemson, South Carolina, United States**

**Abstract** – In live sporting events, varied lighting and weather conditions combined with display and camera gamut differences prevent the application of traditional approaches for managing the representation of brand colors on screen. To overcome these limitations, we use machine learning to identify and color correct specific pixels in every video frame without affecting non-brand colors while also automatically adjusting to changes in lighting, weather conditions, and camera angle. The resulting patented algorithm, named ColorNet, is trained on thousands of paired examples of color-correct and color-incorrect frames pulled from broadcast footage of Clemson football games. The first iteration of ColorNet (ColorNet 1.0) successfully performed real-time color correction for Clemson University's orange (RGB 245 102 0) at 60 frames per second (fps). The next challenge was to expand the original ColorNet model to simultaneously correct multiple brand colors without sacrificing speed and accuracy. The model architecture was modified in order to accommodate the more complex task of correcting two brand colors at once. The resulting algorithm (ColorNet 1.5) performs real-time color correction for two brand colors simultaneously and in real time. Concerns arose during this phase of development that compression artifacts might be affecting model training and performance. This led to a series of tests comparing model performance when using MP4 compressed vs MXF uncompressed video formats in the training process. Ultimately, these tests showed that MP4 compression does not negatively impact model performance. This presentation will share the results of the expanded algorithm and the compression format tests.

## Introduction

Artificial intelligence (AI) refers to a broad spectrum of algorithms that computer systems use to perform tasks that have previously required a human level of intelligence to accomplish. These techniques have already been absorbed into a variety of industries ranging from music recommendations to smart mirrors that display personalized information [1]. Artificial intelligence also has the potential to revolutionize the field of graphic communications and is already being used to automate operations within printing companies [2] and provide AI-powered creative tools in image editing [3, 4]. Commercially, AI has also been successfully used to accurately target appropriate demographics in digital marketing [5].

A common problem within the broadcasting world is the accurate representation of brand coloring in live video. Inconsistencies caused by ambient lighting, screen and camera technology, weather conditions, gamut limitations, and many other factors result in variance in visual accuracy of brand colors. Currently, this is handled manually by a technician who attempts to correct sometimes dozens of incoming camera feeds all in real-time. To assist in this process, the white balance for each camera is set to a predetermined value prior to the event and the technician controls knobs for brightness and

This paper is excerpted from the Proceedings of the 2021 NAB Broadcast Engineering and Information Technology (BEIT) Conference, © 2021, National Association of Broadcasters, 1 M Street S.E., Washington, DC 20003 USA.

red, green, and blue values, adjusting the overall color of video feeds throughout the event. While this is successful in minimizing differences between cameras, sweeping adjustments like this are prone to impact more than just affected areas and often distort the non-brand colors [6]. This is important because studies have shown that visual consistency and accuracy of colors are correlated with the consumers' connection with the brand, which is a significant aspect of viewing a live event [7].

In a new approach to this problem, ColorNet was developed, using a specific type of artificial intelligence known as machine learning. The machine learning model was trained on color-correct and incorrect frames that were pulled from broadcast footage of a Clemson University football game where the orange in the broadcast appeared inaccurate. The color-correct frames were created using Adobe Premiere Pro and the Lumetri Color Panel, where a color matte of Clemson's brand color orange, Pantone 165, was imported as a reference for manually color correcting frames. As a result, ColorNet automatically targets only the appropriate pixels within each frame, see Figure 1.

FIGURE 1: A COLOR INACCURATE VIDEO FRAME ON THE LEFT, A COLOR CORRECTED FRAME IN THE MIDDLE, AND A CORRECTION MASK ON THE RIGHT.

Compared to other machine learning models, which are typically complex with millions of parameters, the first iteration of ColorNet only contained 62 free parameters allowing for the quick corrections necessary in real-time video. An alpha test was completed at Clemson University, where a live football broadcast was split and a duplicate feed was passed through the ColorNet model and streamed onto the jumbotron in the basketball arena to simulate how the model would correct during a live event. A beta test was successfully completed with an audience during a live basketball game in Littlejohn Coliseum. After completing these tests, the next step in model development was training another version of ColorNet, version 1.5, with the goal of simultaneously correcting for two brand colors, Clemson purple and Clemson orange. This was the first time the model was addressing the complexity of correcting for two colors at once.

## Methods and Materials

### Correcting Multiple Colors

The first step in creating a new model capable of correcting Clemson orange and purple was expanding the training dataset to include examples that demonstrate both purple and orange color correction. The training dataset for the original ColorNet consisted of footage from a single rainy night game, where every 14$^{th}$ frame was sampled, yielding 4,291 frames. One-fifth of the frames were withheld to test the accuracy of the model, while the remaining frames were used for training. The expanded dataset added footage where both Clemson purple and Clemson orange brand colors were being corrected. The 2019 Clemson versus Wofford football game was used for these tests because Clemson wore purple jerseys for Military Appreciation week. A challenge of correcting for purple was finding available training data, as Clemson traditionally wears purple at only one football game each season. The Wofford clips provided 3214 images total, with 514 of these images withheld for testing the model.

Due to ColorNet's simple network architecture, the model had difficulty training on the expanded dataset. It became clear that the network architecture would have to be modified in order to perform well on the task of correcting two colors concurrently. In this work, we present a modified neural network architecture, ColorNet 1.5, designed with the flexibility to handle a more complex range of color correction scenarios.

The primary difference between ColorNet 1.5 and the ColorNet 1.0 is the addition of more convolutional layers and the use of residual connections between successive layers of the network, see Figure 2. These modifications give the network the higher representational capacity needed for the more complex task of correcting several colors simultaneously. This comes at the cost of additional free parameters: 1469 compared to the 62 of the original ColorNet. Despite this increase, ColorNet 1.5 is still much simpler than many commonly used neural network architectures. For comparison, the popular ResNet-50 architecture has roughly 23 million free parameters [8].

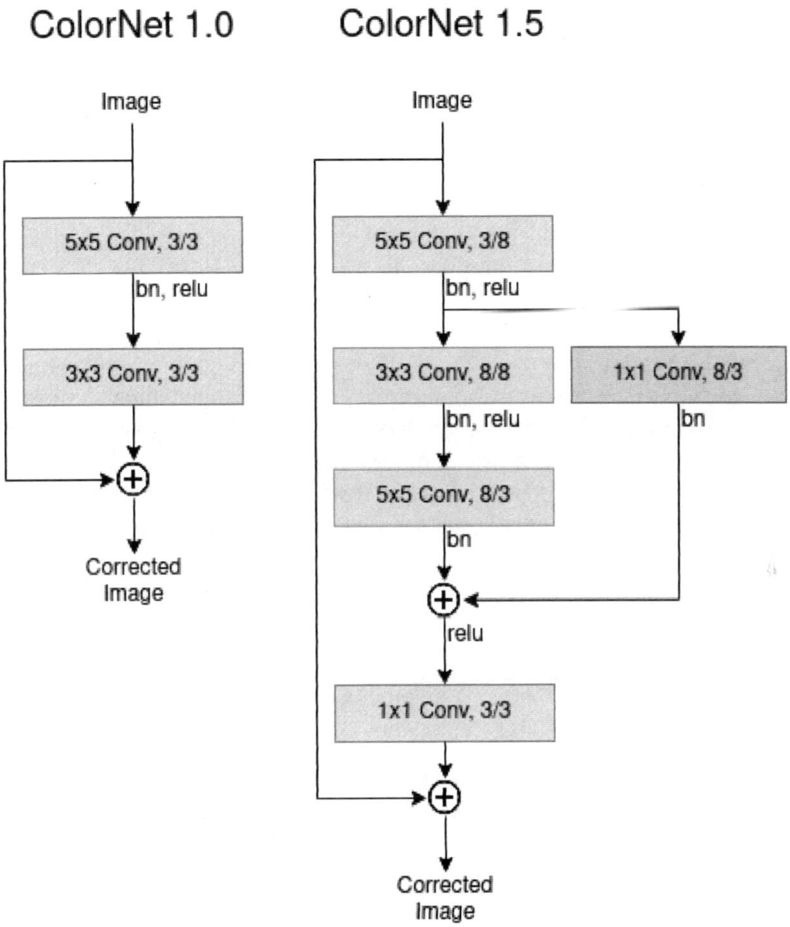


FIGURE 2: ARCHITECTURE DIAGRAMS FOR THE ORIGINAL COLORNET MODEL AND COLORNET 1.5. THE LATTER ARCHITECTURE ADDS AN ADDITIONAL RESNET-STYLE BLOCK BETWEEN THE INPUT AND OUTPUT CONVOLUTIONS. EACH BLOCK REPRESENTS A CONVOLUTION OPERATION OVER THE INPUTS. THE FIRST SET OF NUMBERS ON EACH BLOCK REPRESENTS THE KERNEL SIZE. THE SECOND SET REPRESENTS THE NUMBER OF INPUT AND OUTPUT CHANNELS, RESPECTIVELY.

## Compression Tests

During the process of finding a model architecture that would work on the expanded dataset, questions arose about whether compression artifacts in the training data, see Figure 3, make it more difficult for the model to converge on a solution. In some cases, the scale of the compression artifacts is similar to the scale of the color corrections as measured in pixel intensity. This introduces significant spurious signals into the model at training time which could potentially harm the model's ability to learn the underlying desired patterns of color correction. On the other hand, it might be that the training process is stable to such noise perturbations leading to little or no effect on the final performance.

FIGURE 3: A MASK GENERATED FROM COMPRESSED FOOTAGE ON THE LEFT AND A MASK GENERATED FROM UNCOMPRESSED FOOTAGE ON THE RIGHT.

The frames used as training data for ColorNet and Colornet 1.5 were JPGs pulled from MP4 video files, both of which are compressed file formats. To test whether compression was negatively impacting the model training, a subset of the training data was isolated to compare model training and performance on compressed versus uncompressed footage. The 2018 Clemson versus Louisville football game footage was used for testing because of the difficulty ColorNet had distinguishing between Clemson Orange and Louisville Red on this dataset. A challenging test case magnifies the potential impact compression artifacts have on model performance. To isolate potential weakness in the model architecture from the impact of noise, the more complex ColorNet 1.5 architecture was used for running compression tests. Two versions of ColorNet 1.5 were trained using 3598 training images and 1080 validation images--the first version using compressed JPG frames pulled from MP4 video files and the second using uncompressed PNG frames pulled from MXF video files.

To further quantify the impact of JPG compression on image quality, a baseline error was calculated for the compressed and uncompressed datasets. The Mean Absolute Error was calculated between an uncorrected input image and the manually corrected counterpart, over all of the frames in the Louisville validation dataset. This baseline error serves as a threshold to ensure that there is not more error being introduced by the model than the amount of error that we are trying to fix in the first place. In addition, since the compressed and uncompressed data are of similar perceptual quality, it is more relevant to evaluate the model's performance relative to these baselines rather than in absolute units.

## Results and Discussion

### Correcting Multiple Colors

The success of ColorNet 1.5 at correcting both purple and orange is a positive indicator that similar processes could be used to train a model for a variety of brand colors. Figure 4 shows ColorNet 1.0 and ColorNet 1.5 performance when attempting to correct multiple colors. As seen in the examples, ColorNet 1.0 failed to simultaneously correct for two colors, only recognizing how to correct Clemson orange. Whereas the ColorNet 1.5 architecture succeeded in correcting both Clemson's purple and orange brand colors.

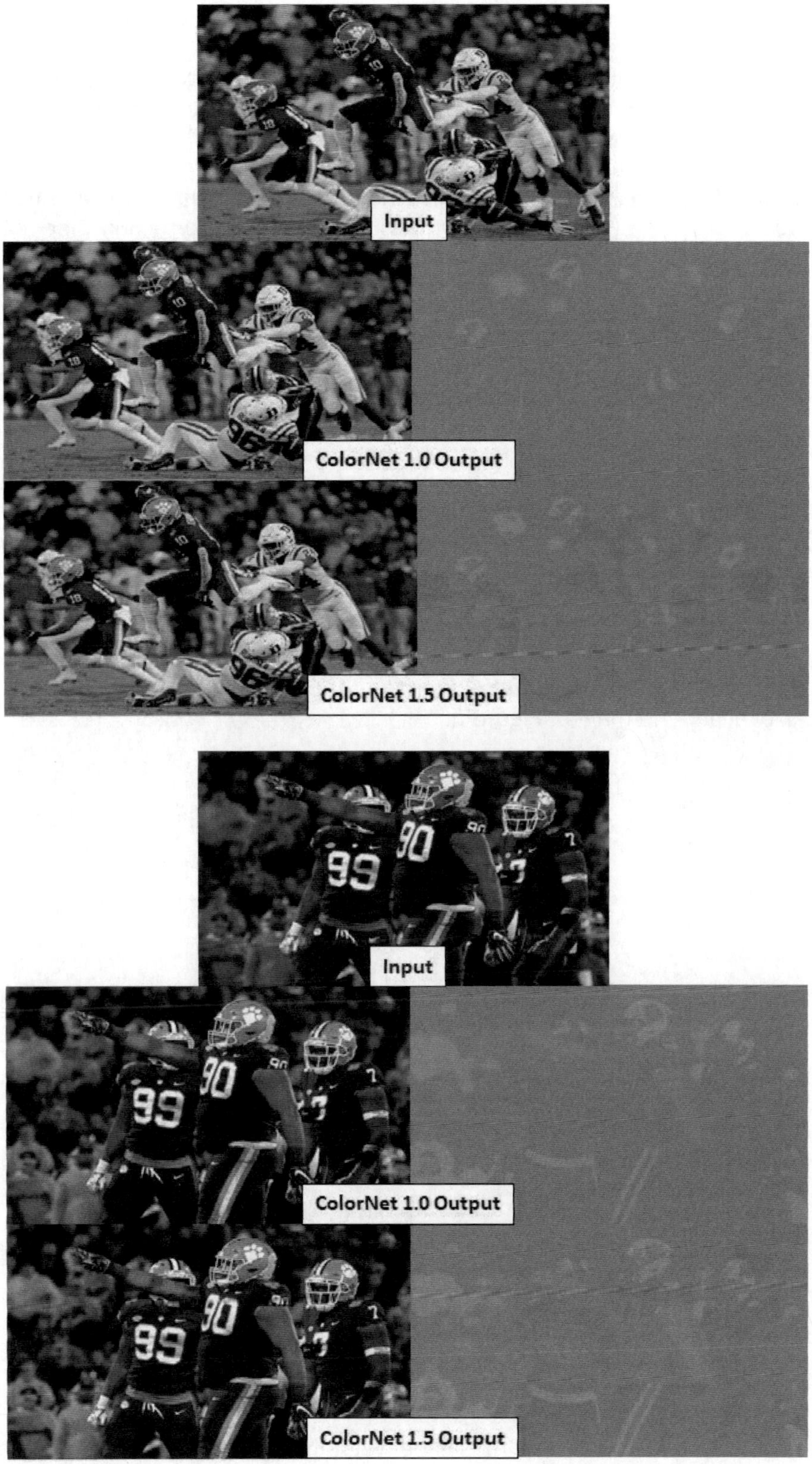


FIGURE 4: COLORNET 1.0 VERSUS COLORNET 1.5 PERFORMANCE ON THE EXPANDED DATASET.

The new model was able to perform natural looking color correction for both purple and orange, shifting the hue of the helmets and jerseys to brand specification while maintaining the visual subtleties of the image such as the highlights on the helmets and shadows on the jerseys. Maintaining these features is important for preventing the color correction from appearing artificial or exaggerated. Quantitatively, when testing on three training attempts of thirty epochs each, ColorNet 1.0 achieved a best test loss (MAE) of 0.0641. ColorNet 1.5 was able to achieve a best test loss of 0.0595. Upon examining the correction masks, ColorNet 1.5 is successful at avoiding color adjustments in most unwanted regions of the image, such as the grass. However, as seen in past models when correcting Clemson orange, ColorNet 1.5 struggled to distinguish between warm skin tones and certain shades of orange, leading to color correction in unwanted areas. Another challenge the model encountered was recognizing the difference between Clemson's jersey colors and an opposing team's uniform when they wore similar brand colors. Future steps for the research plan to address this issue by creating a generalized color correction model using image segmentation that could specify and target all possible team colors.

### Compression Tests

As anticipated, the baseline error for the JPG image format was much higher than the baseline error for the PNG format, with test loss (MAE) values of 0.0490 and 0.0316 respectively. After running three trains of thirty epochs each for both the compressed and uncompressed files, the results clearly showed that the shifted baseline error caused the uncompressed image MXF footage to converge to a lower overall error. The best epoch for the compressed footage resulted in an MAE value of 0.0359, whereas the best value for uncompressed footage was significantly lower at 0.0182. Taking these numbers at face value seems to indicate that MXF footage performs notably better than MP4 footage. However, when the baseline error is subtracted from the MAE values, the models are actually training to a near identical level of performance, Figure 5.

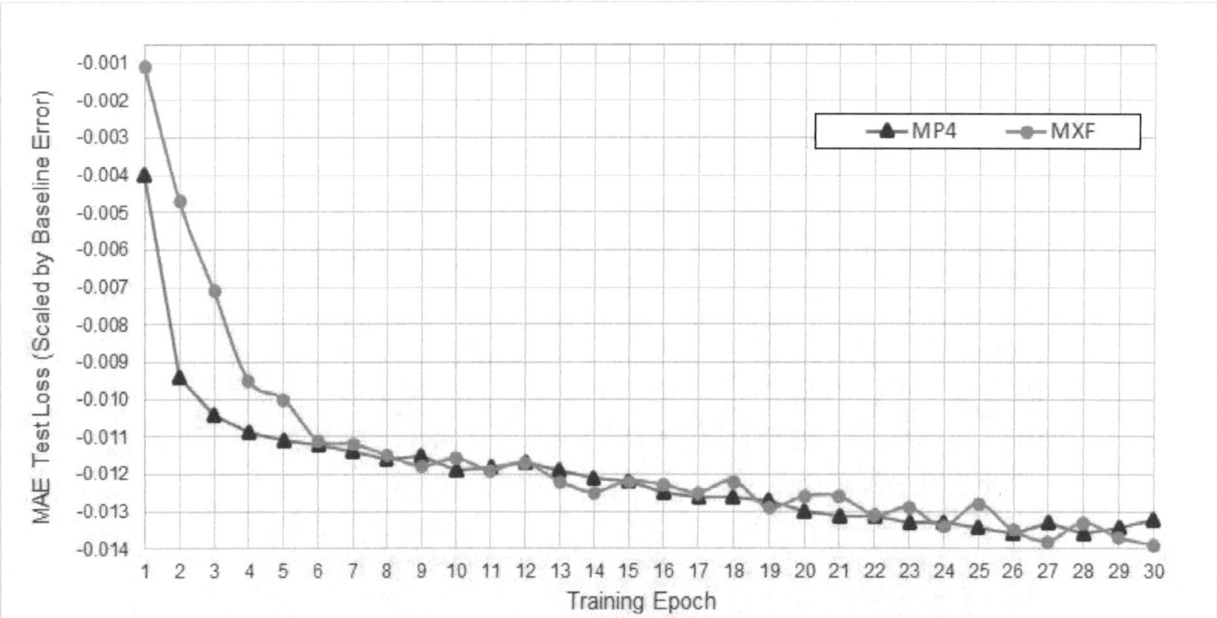


FIGURE 5: MP4 VS MXF LOSS OVER TIME WITH COLORNET 1.5.

In addition, when comparing the qualitative results between the models trained on compressed and uncompressed footage, the visual appearance of the color correction is almost indistinguishable, as seen in Figure 5.

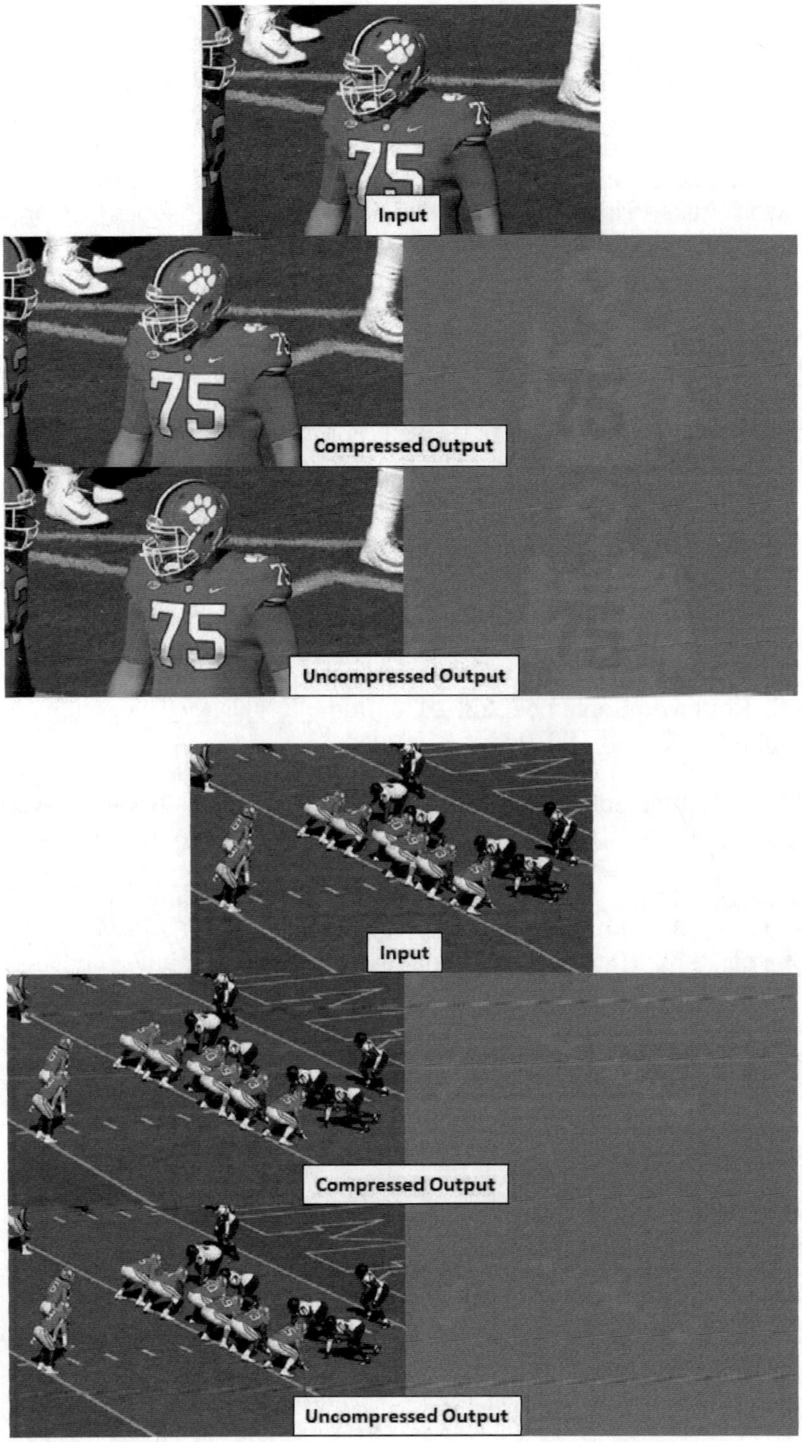


FIGURE 5: VISUAL PERFORMANCE WHEN TRAINING ON COMPRESSED VERSUS UNCOMPRESSED FOOTAGE.

## Conclusions

By examining model convergence rates between uncompressed and compressed footage, the noise due to training on compressed footage did not hinder model performance. The compression artifacts shifted the baseline error, making compressed footage produce higher test error that did not actually correlate with declines in visual performance. In addition, using uncompressed data makes the data preparation process much more arduous, as uncompressed files take up an enormous amount of storage space. For example, a two-minute 59.94 (60) FPS MP4 clip is 148 MB, and a two minute 59.94 (60) FPS MXF clip is 3.2 GB. Model training time is also worse for uncompressed data. For example, training a ColorNet 1.5 model on uncompressed footage from a single football game took around 2.5 times longer than it would take to train the same model on compressed footage. Considering all factors, the team decided to continue using compressed training footage in further model development.

The ColorNet 1.5 architecture demonstrates that models are capable of correcting a wider variety of brand colors than Clemson orange. This provides evidence that similar approaches would be transferable for correcting any desired set of brand colors, as long as the required amount of training data was available containing the additional colors. However, this caveat of needing to train new models for each added brand color is an arduous task. For this reason, a new ColorNet 2.0 model is under development that employs image segmentation to create a football color correction model that should work for any team color without the need for additional training data for each desired color.

## References


[1] Chethan K., Adnan A., Nikhil G., Pragathi N. S., Sourabh K., "Artificial Intelligence Based Smart Mirror." *International Journal of Innovative Technology and Exploring Engineering (IJITEE)*, 8(6S4). 2019, pp.468-472. Retrieved September 28, 2020, from https://www.ijitee.org/wp-content/uploads/papers/v8i6s4/F10970486S419.pdf

[2] Davidson, A., 2017. "Automated Artificial Intelligence Revolutionizes Printing." Retrieved September 28, 2020, from https://blog.konicaminolta.us/automated-artificial-intelligence-revolutionizes-printing/.

[3] Adobe Communications Team., "Adobe Named One of Fast Company's 'Most Innovative Companies' for AI." (2018, Febuary 20), Retrieved November 12, 2020, from https://blog.adobe.com/en/2018/02/20/adobe-named-one-fast-companys-innovative-companies-ai.html.

[4] Jain, D. "A Glimpse Under the Hood of Adobe's AI and ML Innovations: Adobe Sensei ML Framework." *Adobe Tech Blog*. Retrieved November 1, 2019, from https://medium.com/adobetech/a-glimpse-under-the-hood-of-adobes-ai-and-ml-innovations-54c8155801a8.

[5] Lou, Q., Sarkhel, S., Mitra, S. and Swaminathan, V., "Content-based effectiveness prediction of video advertisements." *IEEE International Symposium on Multimedia (ISM).* pp. 69-72. Retrieved December 1, 2020, from https://arxiv.org/pdf/2008.03274.pdf.

[6] Mayes, E., Lineberger, J. P., Mayer, M., Sanborn, A., Smith, H., & Walker, E., "Automated Brand Color Accuracy for Realtime Video." *SMPTE Motion Imaging Journal*, *130*(3). 2021, pp. 45–49. https://doi.org/10.5594/JMI.2021.3058397.

[7] Chang, W.L. and Lin, H.L., "The impact of color traits on corporate branding." *African Journal of Business Management*, 4(15). 2010, pp. 3344-3355. Retrieved September 28, 2020, from https://academicjournals.org/journal/AJBM/article-full-text-pdf/CF287D320855.

[8] He, K., Zhang, X., Ren, S., & Sun, J., "Deep residual learning for image recognition." *Proceedings of the IEEE conference on computer vision and pattern recognition,* 2016, pp. 770-778.

# Handling Event-Based Frame Rate Conversion in OTT Streaming Services

**Paola Hobson**
**InSync Technology Ltd**
**Petersfield, Hants, United Kingdom**
enquiries@insync.tv

**Valentijn Siebrands**
**M2A Media**
**London, United Kingdom**

**Abstract** – A streaming service needs frame rate conversion (standards conversion) to manage the multiple delivery formats and frame rates for different regions and countries. This paper explains how a fully responsive on-demand cloud service that includes on-demand software frame rate conversion was evaluated by a leading sports streaming platform. The streaming platform's feedback and comments about how standards conversion can be improved for future deployment provide valuable insight into emerging pay-per-use cloud services.

## Introduction

Broadcasters and media companies engaged in live international content distribution are familiar with the need for standards conversion. Multiple broadcast frame rates and formats are in use throughout the world, and with an ever-growing number of standards to support in mobile and streaming services, high quality, live, standards conversion is an essential part of many businesses.

OTT streaming service providers are no different. OTT delivery workflows deliver localized broadcast grade streams to a myriad of devices globally. Typically, these workflows run fully in the public cloud, receiving mezzanine quality transport streams from playout, and inserting dynamic content to produce localized versions, where reformatting, transcoding, packaging, encrypting and delivering to CDN are entirely located in the cloud. For international coverage, frame rate conversion between 50 and 59Hz is commonly needed. For example, US Football acquired at 59Hz needs frame rate conversion to 50Hz for European viewers. When streaming live sports, very high-quality frame rate conversion is essential to ensure all viewers obtain the best possible experience.

On-premise and/or hardware frame rate converters break the workflow and result in operational costs (as well as capital expenditure) which reduces the economics of a service. In this paper, we show how streamed sports services can be monetized globally in a highly cost-effective workflow, where frame rate conversion is available on-demand in a fully cloud-enabled process. This unique new concept is enabled by flexibility and scalability of cloud-enabled software and development of highly responsive mechanisms for service spin-up and tear-down.

This paper is excerpted from the Proceedings of the 2021 NAB Broadcast Engineering and Information Technology (BEIT) Conference, © 2021, National Association of Broadcasters, 1 M Street S.E., Washington, DC 20003 USA.

## International Content Workflows

Live and on-demand, over-the-top video streaming services enable international audiences to enjoy real-time events happening in any location. Live sporting events are often the most popular, but also often involve the most complexity, with delayed starts, over-runs and last-minute schedule changes being just a few of the challenges faced by sports producers.

In a typical workflow, similar to the example shown in Figure 1, content from live events produced around the world will be handed off via pre-booked links to production studios, where the content is localized. Such localization can include local language commentary and audio description, the addition of graphics, branding and other overlays, subtitling, SCTE insertion, and profanity removal. The finished program is then handed off to a cloud-based service provider for reformatting, transcoding, packaging, encrypting and delivering to playout and CDN. Transfers into playout services may use satellite, broadband, and more recently IP transport in a public cloud.

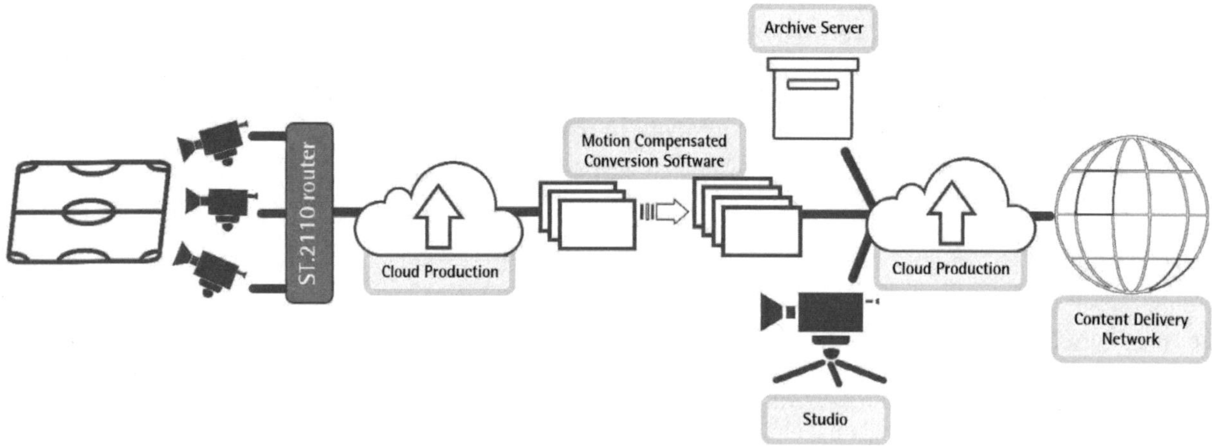


FIGURE 1: EXAMPLE WORKFLOW

At the playout or CDN stage, distribution could be anywhere in the world, so frame rate conversion (standards conversion) is therefore needed in order to manage the multiple delivery formats and frame rates for each region. Where the OTT workflows run fully in the cloud, live cloud-based software standards conversion is therefore needed for the workflow to be entirely cloud-based.

The alternative - attempting to use an on-premise converter - is daunting enough by sheer complexity of the problem, even before the costs are considered. A cloud-based live standards converter avoids the need to transform back to baseband on premise, then re-ingress into the cloud, with all the security, synchronization and latency challenges that entails.

## Event Based Services

A key consideration for sports services is the discontinuous and sometimes irregular nature of sports tournaments. Some events occur on a 4-year cycle (e.g. Olympic Games), some annually (e.g. Tour de France), down to those which happen weekly (e.g. soccer leagues). Sporting events can be seasonal (e.g. skiing in winter) or irregular (e.g. showcase boxing matches). Keeping a dedicated standards conversion asset on standby can be highly capital intensive, with the return on investment for the purchase being limited by usage of the asset - for example, used at weekends only, or used for 4 weeks for the duration of a tournament then not needed again for several months.

Major events often require multiple simultaneous feeds. For example, during the Wimbledon tennis championship, live coverage of Centre Court plus Courts 1 and 2 is typically expected. With the hardware conversion paradigm, multiple converters will be needed, which also must be sent to the production location, thus incurring capital expenditure and transportation costs, in addition to the logistical nightmare of finding space, power and cooling for all the equipment.

A cost-effective and practical solution for events-based service providers is to locate the standards conversion in the cloud, as illustrated in Figure 2.

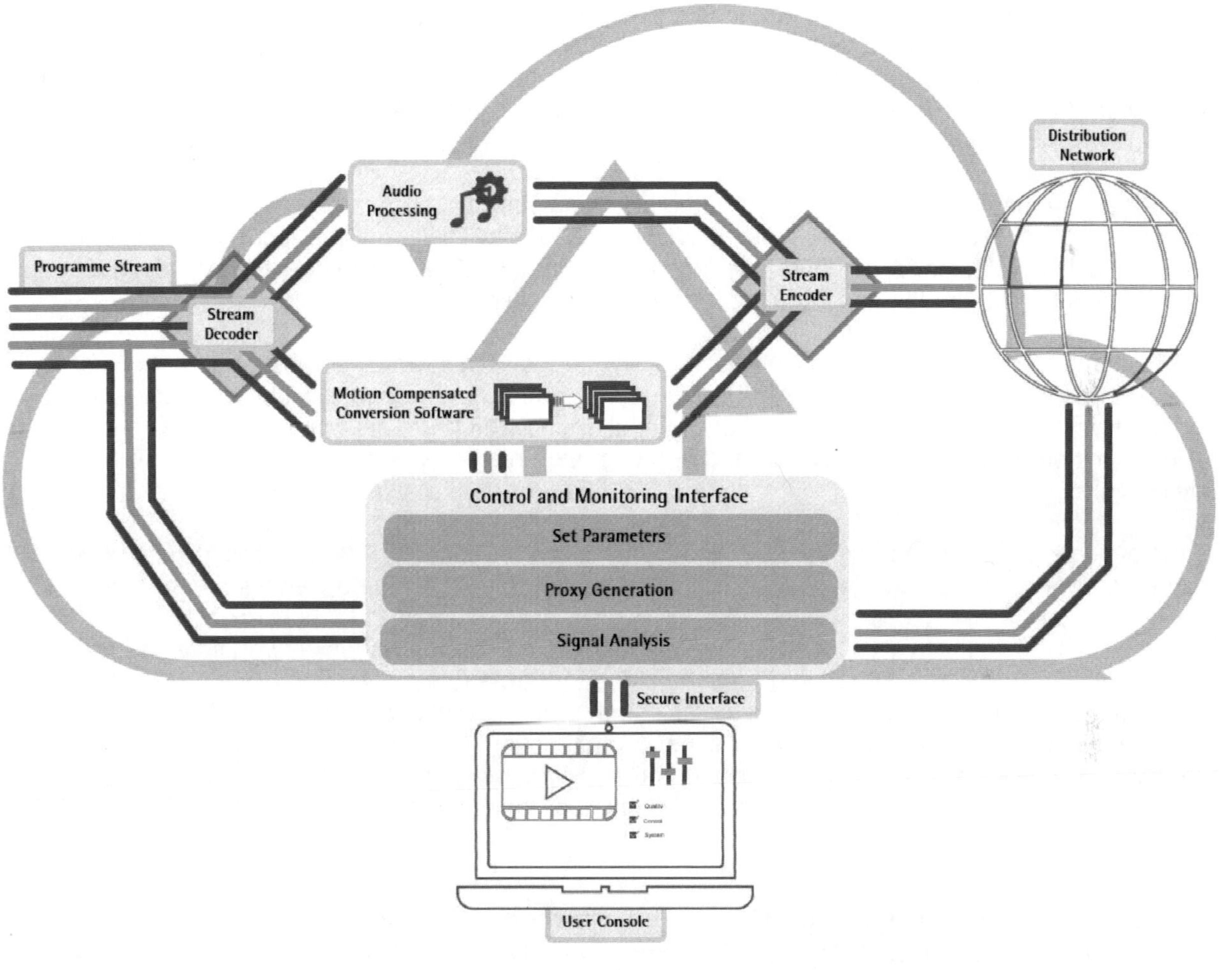


FIGURE 2: WORKFLOW WITH STANDARDS CONVERSION IN THE CLOUD

The workflow of Figure 2 is only possible if the motion compensated standards converter is a pure software converter using CPU-only resources. GPU-based converters, with their reliance on specific hardware elements, do not have the same flexibility in being always deployable, on any instance in any region. Cloud services, such as those provided by M2A Media, have the further advantage that customers only pay for workflow processes when they need them, so potential capital expenditure on permanent physical hardware assets can be replaced with operating expenditure which is only charged when the event is live.

Cloud-based standards conversion further supports the event workflow model in that the processing can be accessed from any location within the broadcaster's contribution or delivery chain, since physical content delivery via BNCs in the hardware model, is replaced by logical signal flow into software input/output processes. This allows the converter to be a shared resource available for any event, worldwide without transportation costs or logistics.

## Technical Evaluation

### Background – Sports Production

In a typical sports production environment, international content is delivered to a local studio, where graphics, commentary and captions are added. The program then continues its journey into the playout network and will be delivered to playout centers and CDNs. Increasingly, broadcasters and sports rights holders are taking advantage of cloud-based pay-per-use services to support their operational needs. With hundreds of events taking place around the world on a daily basis, the scale of operations should not be underestimated.

M2A Media are innovators in cloud-based video solutions offering broadcasters and sports rights owners smart orchestration tools to manage live video at scale. Their services orchestrate the end-to-end AWS resources needed to support the required thousands of live events each week. Services runs fully redundantly with on demand capacity management, scaling and monitoring.

M2A Live and Connect [1] provide highly reliable, low latency live streams across a huge number of devices for several sports broadcasters. They enable dynamic autoscaling in order to meet spikes in demand from hundreds to millions of viewers without impacting QoS. This gives each customer great flexibility in their international production and end-user experience, which would not be possible using satellite links.

As the provider of OTT head-end services to several sports broadcasters, M2A Media's suite of cloud-based products have enabled the delivery of live event streams, at scale, to viewers around the world.

As discussed above, until very recently, the missing link in a fully cloud-enabled workflow was frame rate conversion. Breaking a stream out from the cloud for frame rate conversion using on-premise hardware then re-ingesting for delivery is inefficient, and has issues of synchronization and security, with potential for loss of quality. The sheer scale of multi-channel operation means replication of hardware, with associated costs, power consumption, and physical real-estate. Therefore, integration of FrameFormer software standards conversion within M2A Connect provides an interesting alternative for international OTT services.

### International Content Distribution – A New Experiment

DAZN is a leading international OTT sports provider, handling over 30,000 live events per year. Their streams are available in more than 200 countries and territories, connecting global fans to their favourite sports, with rights ownership for a wide range of different sports. Being an early adopter of new technologies, their continuous innovation enables them to stay ahead in live and on-demand streaming, with a focus on delivering the best user experience.

DAZN's channels reach millions of monthly users in multiple languages, so a finished program may be delivered to a single end point, or multiple destinations, where different formats and frame rates may be needed. For example, the UEFA Women's Champions League matches will be produced in 50Hz since it originates in Europe, but viewers in Japan or USA will need a 59Hz version.

With this array of variables in mind, DAZN agreed to evaluate frame rate conversion in the cloud. Since the majority of their workflows are cloud-based, FrameFormer by InSync Technology Ltd was an obvious choice for experimentation with a new workflow.

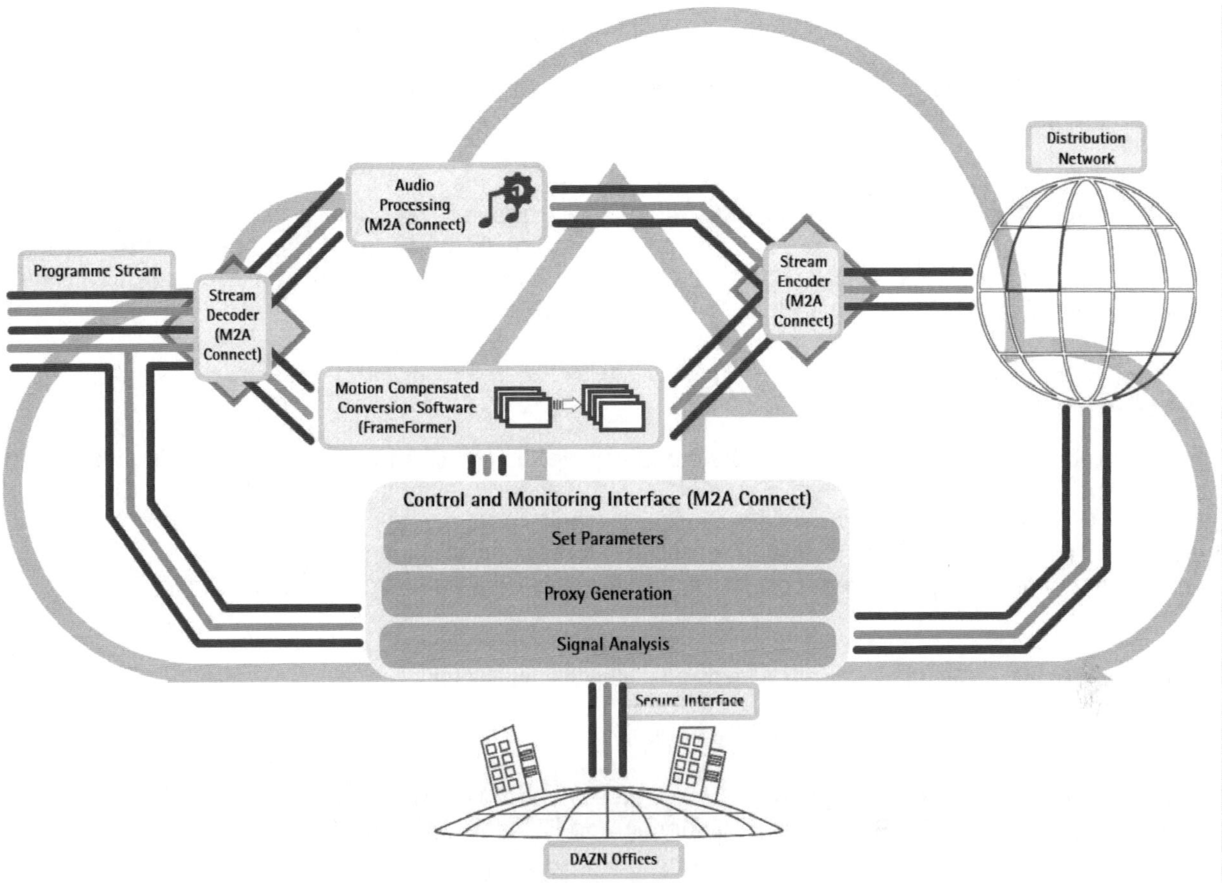


FIGURE 3: WORKFLOW EXPERIMENTATION

Reduction of motion compensated standards conversion to a real-time cloud-enabled deployment, without compromising picture quality, was a key achievement which has enabled the addition of this process into a cloud streaming workflow. As explained in our previous paper [2], live motion compensated standards conversion in the cloud is now possible. This has been achieved through development of highly efficient algorithms and finely tuned task management which enables real-time, live frame rate conversion to run on CPU-instances. In this way, the highest possible quality standards conversion can be flexibly deployed on a range of processing targets, including cloud instances which can be spun up and torn down according to live sports events schedules.

## Frame Rate Conversion Experimentation

For evaluation of frame rate conversion, many broadcasters collate a set of typical sports clips, which are representative of their popular sports services, for example soccer, rugby, motor racing and curling. With many years of experience in international content provision, video experts choose a selection of material which is known to stretch the performance of standards converters. Picture quality is an essential element in viewer satisfaction, and these experts know what artifacts to look for in their converted material.

Typical standards conversions require steps of deinterlacing, temporal rate conversion and rescaling. Most broadcasters' content includes both interlaced and progressive material, thus allowing experts to validate FrameFormer's deinterlacing quality. The deinterlacer must preserve the maximum possible picture resolution and introduce zero (or in practice a minimal level of) artifacts, since downstream processing stages will effectively magnify any tiny picture defects that may be introduced [3]. FrameFormer uses a number of non-linear processes, including perceptually adaptive algorithms, which cleanly manage deinterlacing to create smooth lines and continuous textures, whilst preserving the maximum possible resolution and sharpness.

To exercise FrameFormer's temporal rate conversion, DAZN chose a variety of complex and fast-moving content. Conversions between 50Hz and 59Hz were tested, on compressed material. Motion compensated frame rate conversion, such as that provided by FrameFormer, is needed for the highest possible picture quality when sports content is converted. Alternatives such as frame repeat/duplication or linear conversion led to blurring, judder, and loss of resolution.

## Conclusions

A highly flexible frame rate conversion in the cloud was set up by M2A Media for DAZN to evaluate, incorporating FrameFormer by InSync Technology Ltd. The innovative service, entitled M2A Connect Cloud Frame Rate Converter, enables events-based standards conversion to be available on a pay-per-use basis in the cloud. Such provision represents a break-through in SaaS offerings, as it enables management of thousands of events every week in a highly cost-effective and reliable manner.

## References


[1] M2A Connect https://m2amedia.tv/m2a-connect/

[2] Hobson, P., "Is the Technology Ready Yet for Live Standards Conversion in The Cloud?", Proceedings of the 2020 Broadcast Engineering and IT Conference, 13 May 2020.

[3] Hobson, P., "Format and Standards Conversion", in National Association of Broadcasters Engineering Handbook, February 2018 (ISBN 9781138930513).

# How to Maximize Hybrid Cloud Capabilities for the "New Normal"

**Julián Fernández-Campón Montero**
**Tedial**
**Málaga, Spain**
jfcampon@tedial.com

**Abstract** – The Covid-19 pandemic has accelerated many processes that normally would have taken years to mature. The near-global lockdown forced entire companies to adjust overnight to a new work paradigm that included remote operation based on Cloud computing. But now, months later, with time to review, 20/20 hindsight and a clear vision of what has been done and how, it's time to realistically think about what can and what cannot be achieved remotely, and, most importantly, how to develop contingency plans and define a consistent and realistic roadmap toward cloud operations.

A Hybrid cloud solution allows customers to transition to the cloud at their own pace and with less risk. Hybrid cloud infrastructure follows the basic principle of "bringing applications to media" and not "media to applications". By using computing storage and services architecture that combine the privacy and security of a private cloud with the scalability and elasticity of a public cloud, users benefit from orchestration among various platforms and multiple sites. The users can perform regular operations using high-resolution content on-premise inside a secure IT environment that is not accessible from outside their facility and that is fully under the control of their IT team. Less critical operations including burst or peak demands in business operations can be quickly deployed and run in the cloud for enhanced agility.

In addition, some operations that need to be executed on-premise require continuous access to media. Other operations (e.g., AI tools) that use cloud services can be quickly deployed and run in the cloud for enhanced agility. This means that media companies pay only for the period of time required by the additional business operations. High-cost services such as storage for archiving can benefit from the ability to tailor the operations to the business cost criteria.

In this paper we'll address the main challenges that could be encountered, and we'll discuss the solutions that will ensure a smooth and seamless transition and protect business continuity.

## Hybrid Cloud Use Cases

Hybrid Cloud can be used for multiple use cases:

- Multisite workflows where operation is split between different locations
- Use of AI tools to enrich local content
- Remote operation
- Maximize content accessibility
- Substantial content distribution - using AI services to scale up and down as required

If we think about it, what all these use cases have in common is that broadcasters can extend in some way their operation (in volume or in features) without paying all the time for the extra services they are not using while at the same time the day to day or the 'stable' operation can be running on-prems with the resources they have acquired. Some studies also reveal that the cost of the cloud can be higher if the use is constant over time, whereas it is more cost effective when the operation is not homogeneous and there are peaks where lots of resources needs to be spin up. In these situations it makes sense to implement a hybrid cloud infrastructure as the infrastructure does not have to be dimensioned for the worst case. Microsoft [1] and NetApp [2] show the cost comparisons between on-prems and cloud deployments.

## Challenges

To maximize Hybrid Cloud capabilities, the system must be configured efficiently taking full advantage of each infrastructure, which means that there are different services and systems to be used on each site. In addition, it has to include all the applications and systems that are going to use the workflows as well as all the storage locations across the different sites.

What are the challenges when implementing a real-world Hybrid Cloud deployment?
The first challenge is point-to-point integration:

- Each system in the platform has a different API
- Each system needs to understand each other
- Changes in one component affects other components
- It can be difficult to maintain and evolve – if one system changes an API for example, it will affect all the other systems

The second challenge is media location and technologies:

- Different technologies and access methods
- Minimize media movements
- Workflows need to be media location aware

The third challenge is multisite workflows:

- Minimize media movement between cloud and on-prems
- Local media management capabilities
- Global management and monitoring to have metrics, reports and the capability to optimize the workflows as needed.

These challenges can be solved, and a Hybrid Cloud platform can be deployed but it will face two important disadvantages:

- Time to Deploy. The integration of all the applications and the workflows configurations is complex and will take some time
- Flexibility, Future Proof. Due to the complexity, changes and adaptations to new business needs will take time and will not be done. The platform will follow the principle of *'if it ain't broke, don't fix it'*.

## Enter the Media Integration Platform

### What is an Integration Platform?

According to Wikipedia [3], *"An integration platform is software which integrates different applications and services. It differentiates itself from the enterprise application integration which has a focus on supply chain management. It uses the idea of system integration to create an environment for engineers."*

This looks really cool and has obvious benefits as a single point to access to all the applications in a specific deployment. So it's quite straightforward to integrate all the applications needed, but it has one serious limitation, which is the point to point integration, as shown in figure [1].

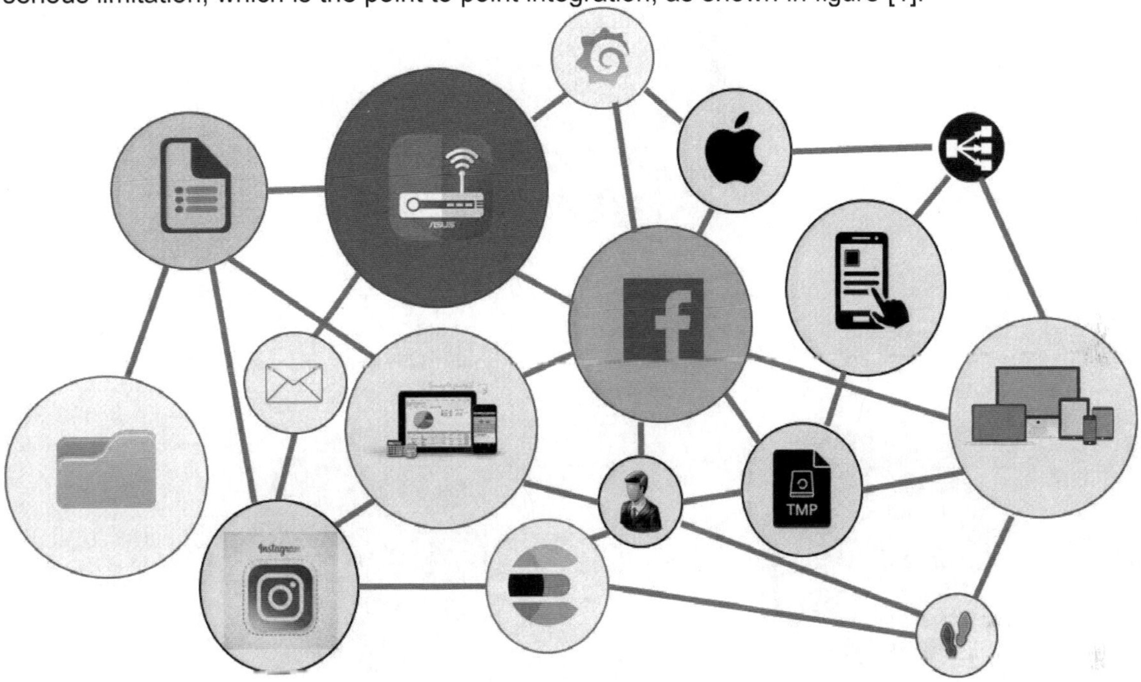


FIGURE 1: INTEGRATION PLATFORM.

Each application that needs to be integrated with another needs to know the API, and so do the proper calls, even though the end point is common, in the Integration platform. Changes in one application will affect to all the applications that are integrated with.
Another limitation of the traditional integration platforms is that they do not manage media; they only manage metadata and control between the different applications. Including the media management adds more complexity to the overall platform.

### Adding Media Management Features: The Media Integration Platform

Adding Media Management features for the integration platform is needed for the broadcast industry, as all the processes in one way or another are managing media. The workflows then need to track the media locations, and the applications will be accessing to that media locations either by analyzing, transforming, delivery, etc.

### The Solution for the Hybrid Cloud

The solution to implement and future proof Hybrid Cloud deployment is a Media Integration Platform, which overcomes these challenges. Using a Media Integration Platform means that there is no point-to-point integration because all the applications are integrated with the Platform.

The Media Integration Platform is based in three pillars. First, it provides a Common Workspace, which allows all the applications to be accessible to the media and not the media delivered to the applications. This is crucial. Second, it has a Common Interface, so all the applications present the same methods. Third, it includes a Normalized Data Model, so all the applications speak the same language.

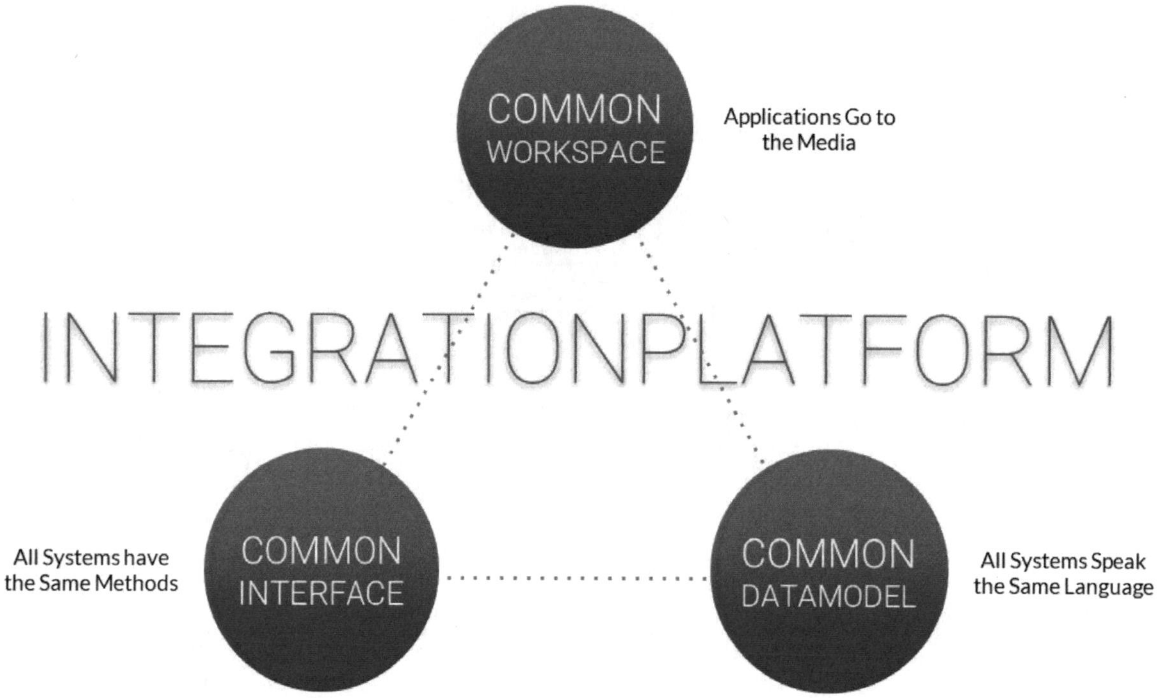


FIGURE 2: MEDIA INTEGRATION PLATFORM PILLARS.

### Common Workspace

- Adds an additional layer of security as it prevents the original media from ever being modified
- Provides a place for all temporary media to be stored
- Defines a set of normalized files so that the application knows what other files will be stored here
- Optimized for each site – on cloud or on-prems
- Offers global management features – quotas, reports etc.
- Provides a Media Location Abstraction which will simplify the definition of the workflows as they are not dependent on the physical media location nor the access methods.

### Common Interface

- All applications to be used in the system present the same method, which is key when configuring workflows. The user can change different applications in the workflow and create new workflows by copying existing ones, or deploy new workflows in the cloud or on-prems
- Same methods will have the same name: Transcode, Analyze, SentTo, and GetFrom
- This leads to workflow simplicity

- Workflows will be future-proof because we'll have the freedom to change workflows in the future without requiring complex modifications

### Normalized Data Model

Now that we have a common workspace where all the applications are held, we have a Common Interface to access the temporary media or the original media. This means that all the methods that carry out the same tasks will have the same name, and all applications will speak the same language. This is achieved by defining a Common Data Model. This is the Integration Platform Data Model that contains all the Content Metadata, which is part of the content.

This includes:

- Editorial
- Technical metadata
- Timeline Annotations
- Collections
- Relations
- Dynamic Metadata (eg. QC Status, TX Ready) needed to take decisions on the workflows.
- Workflow simplification
- Future proof and self-sufficiency because the customer doesn't have to carry out complex modifications in the workflow

## Some Real Applications

### Accessing from Anywhere

Business Benefits: Maximizing User Accessibility, Minimizing Content Movement

In this case media is ingested locally, and some dubbing subtitling needs to be done for localization purposes. This takes place in the cloud, where people are connecting from different territories to access the original low-res media to generate a dubbing track in the specific language required. If editing is needed, it can be carried out on-prems using the high-resolution copy. Finally, low-res validation is carried out in the cloud, from the different territories, in order to check that the media that's been generated fits the audience specifications.

The key points in this workflow include:

- The original media is never moved so all the high-res media stays on-prems
- Significant content accessibility from the cloud using cloud services to access the low-res content in the cloud from different locations
- The copy that is generated to be validated is low-res; we do not move the high-res media into the cloud

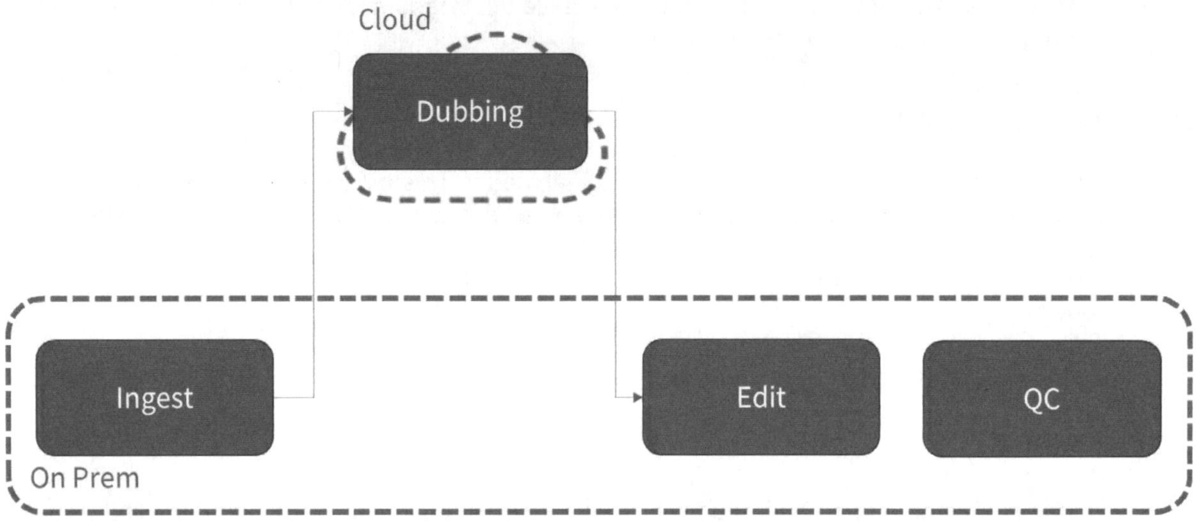


FIGURE 3: LOCALIZATION WORKFLOW.

## Media Local Abstraction

Business Benefits: Same workflows everywhere
Let's now look at the Media Location Abstraction feature of the Media Integration Platform.
All the media stored on the Platform is identified by an ID. The advantage of this is that all the different applications that are being used during the workflow execution don't need to be media aware. All they have to do is request the media ID and the Platform will automatically serve the content from the most suitable location, depending on where the workflow is being executed.

For example, if the workflow is in the cloud, it will open the media from the cloud service, e.g., S3; if the workflow is on-prems, it will serve the media from local storage, e.g., a NAS. Making the workflows independent of the physical location where they're being executed is key. This gives users the visibility and transparency to focus on business strategy.

- Media is identified by an ID
- Abstraction of the Media Location: cloud/on-prems
- Abstraction of the adapters: NFS, S3, Azure etc.
- Workflows don't need to be media aware (unless required)

Following are some examples of applications that require access to the media with different technologies:

- Cloud
  - Transcoding: AWS Elemental
  - AI: AWS Rekognition, Google Vision
- On-Prems:
  - NLE: Adobe CC, Avid Interplay
  - AutoQC: Baton, Vidchecker
  - Transcoding: Vantage

  ...and more...

When we're implementing and configuring these workflows, we don't have to put specific stages in the workflows that are dependent on the location where the workflow is being executed.

### Swappable Applications

Business Benefits: Easy Prototyping, Future Proof

One of the key features of the Media Integration Platform is that we're easily able to change one system for another in order for the system to be future-proof and to provide future workflow evolution. For example, we can have a content enrichment workflow using AI tools where the media is ingested on-prems, enriched in the cloud, and finally edited and validated on-prems. In this case, if for example there are new AI tools that are more suitable to the workflows that we're executing, or we want to test a new AI tool, all we have to do is to change the AI engine. For example, let us say that Google Vision is swapped with AWS Rekognition, but the rest of workflow is unchanged. This is because we have a Common Workspace, we have the Common Interface, and the response given by Google Vision and AWS Rekognition is Normalized.

It's as simple as changing the operation in the workflow:

- The response is normalized to the Media Integration Platform's data model
- The next stage (edit) will be unaffected
- The media location: Google Storage to S3 storage is transparent for the workflow

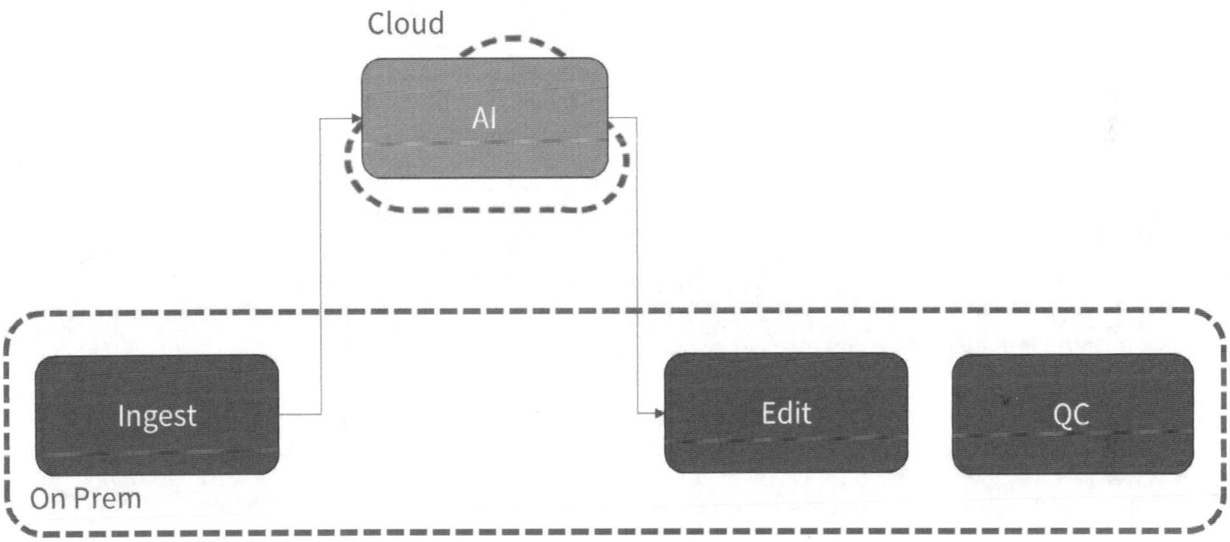


FIGURE 4: SWAPPABLE APPLICATIONS.

## Outcomes

### Outcome 1: Software-Defined Workflows

One of the outcomes, which was highlighted in Movielabs and Hollywood Studios August 2019 "The Future of Media Creation" [4] whitepaper, is Software Defined Workflows. Content production workflows are non-predictable; one does not know in advance how many color corrections or visual effects, for example, are going to be created. This means the workflows must focus on specific production needs, allowing creatives to do everything that they need and not limit their creativity by making them focus on technology. The fact that the technology is future-proof is crucial particularly now that we are living with COVID-19, which causes a lot of uncertainty in terms of production and content generation needs.

- Content Production is iterative, non-predictable
- Focus on the creatives, not on the technology
- Agile to attend Production needs

**Outcome 2: Future Proof**

The platform must be able to evolve quickly to new production needs, to switch between cloud services and on-prems operation, and to provide remote operation. It must adapt quickly to these new requirements. Also, if new content to be produced needs to be optimized in the cloud, it can spin up and down cloud services as and when required. It must be able to evolve to add new applications and new systems, and it must also be able to produce more content efficiently in the future as technology evolves.

- New systems can be swapped easily
- Changes in locations do not affect the workflow logic
- Quick time to market for future needs
- Easy Prototyping
- Interoperability
- Reduced total cost of ownership
- Customers' self-sufficiency

## Conclusion

Hybrid Cloud is the best solution for all the advantages mentioned in this paper. Configuring and deploying an efficient Hybrid Cloud is complex and having a future-proof hybrid cloud is even more complex. This is why having a Media Integration Platform with all the features discussed is absolutely necessary to evolve to new production requirements in the future.

## References

[1] Diamond, Paul. "Cloud Storage vs. on-premise servers:9 things to keep in mind". (*https://www.microsoft.com/en-us/microsoft-365/business-insights-ideas/resources/cloud-storage-vs-on-premises-servers*)

[2] Morgan, Lisa. "On Premise vs Cloud: Key Differences, Cost, Pros & Cons" (*https://www.enterprisestorageforum.com/cloud/on-premise-vs-cloud-storage/*)

[3] Wikipedia, the free encyclopedia. "Integration Platform". (https://en.wikipedia.org/wiki/Integration_platform)

[4] Multiple Authors. "The future of Media Creation". Movielabs (https://movielabs.com/production-technology/)

# Is The Cloud There Yet?

**Peter Wharton**
**TAG Video Systems**
**Tel Aviv, Israel**
peter@tagvs.com

**Abstract** – This paper looks at the advancements that have been made and the challenges that still lie ahead for fully utilizing the cloud in media operations. It examines the "lift and shift" perspective that still pervades most media technology and how cloud utilization is still being held back by operations wedded to legacy workflows. We examine the most recent developments, especially those related to live production in the cloud. This paper also examines two use cases that illustrate how the fully leveraging cloud capabilities can transform media operations. The first looks at how to redesign playout in the cloud for scale while reducing cloud costs to a fraction of the costs of lift and shift. The second use case examines how volumetric cameras and an esports production model could transform live sports production in the cloud.

## The Journey to The Cloud

It's hard to imagine that the first AWS compute instance was launched 15 years ago as a little side business of Amazon. Even as recently as five years ago cloud was still not in the lexicon of most media organizations. Today it's hard to find a media organization that isn't in the middle of a cloud migration initiative. But is the cloud truly there yet for media? And are media organizations truly ready for the cloud and all its potential?

Let's first review why media organizations are moving to the cloud or should consider moving to the cloud. First, moving to the cloud is not a technical decision. The cloud is not simply running your software on someone else's computer. It's not more expensive than running on-premises unless you're not doing it right and you're not including all the relevant factors in your analysis. Yes, most OPEX models have a 36-48 month breakeven to CAPEX purely on a highly simplistic direct cost analysis. But that is too myopic a perspective. It doesn't account for the speed of deployment – or termination – or the cost of the surrounding infrastructure for CAPEX, the expertise needed and concurrent expense to build and maintain facilities, the cost of resiliency, the ease of upgrades and the range of possibility that the cloud opens the door to.

The choice to move to the cloud is ultimately driven by business enablement. It's about preserving capital in a time of great business uncertainty and rapid technological advancements. It's about enabling accelerated adoption of technology to provide business advantage, coupled with rapid deployment to maximize ROI and maintain a competitive edge. It's about creating increased reliability utilizing geographically diverse on-demand resiliency without building expensive backup facilities that loaf along waiting for a disaster to happen. It's about servicing new business models, from the latest OTT platform or live production concept to integrating and divesting of operations to serve ongoing M&A activities. There are many more reasons why media companies are migrating to the cloud, and all these fundamentally serve one fundamental paradigm: to enable the business to thrive in an era of uncertainty and rapid change coupled with an inability to predict the future.

Media organizations have been laggards in migrating to the cloud compared to many other industries. This latency in adoption is the product of several factors: massive processing and bandwidth needed to support current media operations, cloud costs, lack of suitable cloud-enabled media solutions and services, lack of understanding of cloud technology and costs, inability to find the necessary engineering and IT talent to build and manage these systems, and addressing latency caused by remote cloud workflows. One by one these obstacles have been eroded to the point where the cloud is now able to host almost all media operations an organization chooses to migrate.

You can see how these barriers to adoption have fallen. The first at scale deployments in the cloud were for OTT delivery. In 2012, Netflix began the migration of all its delivery from dedicated facilities to AWS. The massive ability to scale on demand and address dynamically changing consumption by an online audience necessitated cloud-based operations. CDNs for media, first launched in the late 1990s, became an integral part of all OTT delivery systems. The delivery mechanisms also improved from transport streams over the internet to Apple's HLS adaptive bit rate streaming in 2009.

By the middle of the last decade, major media companies were beginning to migrate to the cloud in earnest starting with file-based workflows. For file-based workflows, the cloud offered compelling advantages:

- The economics and resilience of cloud storage.
- Transcoding and file processing on-demand, eliminating queues and speeding up workflows.
- Content delivery portals providing direct interchange with suppliers and distributors also in the cloud.
- Frictionless, streamlined, automated metadata-driven end-to-end workflows.

Some of the earliest pioneers of cloud media workflows realized that success in the cloud was more than simply making it work; it was understanding the economics of the cloud before writing the first line of code or creating the first workflow. As a result, they could create media workflow orchestration in the cloud that practically paid for itself through optimization such as:

- Selecting the process used for each media workflow – as an example, one transcoder is not right for all applications.
- Choosing when and where to run a workflow based on cost and availability, especially when leveraging spot instances. Originally spot instances were limited to 15 minutes; today spot instances can be spun up for longer durations such as 1 or 6 hours enabling them to be used for longer duration workflows.
- Highly automated processing creating touchless media workflows that reduce costs while acceleration time to availability.

Towards the end of the last decade, linear workflows such as playout started to migrate to the cloud. Discovery Communications pioneered much of this effort when they started their cloud playout migration in 2016, a project that would take three years to complete and resulted in some 400 channels globally playing out of the cloud. Making realtime linear workflows work in the cloud presented several obstacles:

- Getting compressed transport streams to and from the cloud required protocols that would address packet jitter, packet loss and packet reordering. Tools that used ARQ (RFC 3366) such as Zixi, VideoFlow, SRT and most recently the open source RIST provide the necessary protection albeit with increased latency.
- Running in a shared virtual machine environment introduces challenges in creating a perfectly stable and timed transport stream output. Solutions include underutilizing the instance, bare metal instances and refactoring code.

## Current State of Media in The Cloud

By the end of the decade, playout in the cloud was readily available from many suppliers. The author evaluated 40 such systems for a project and found several that were broadcast-grade including one that was cloud-native. Since then, several more cloud-native playout systems have been developed that meet the needs of broadcasters, as well as countless OTT-specific playout systems and platforms. In the US, several large station groups have begun migration to the cloud. Even though much of their content for the main channel on a station might be generated locally by the news operation, the benefits of moving to the cloud are driven by:

- The OTT and digital delivery side
- Delivery of file-based subchannels (ATSC .2 "diginets")
- Collaborative news workflows across stations
- Unification of playout technologies and workflows across the enterprise

These reasons make a compelling case for cloud migration the same way centralized broadcasting transformed station group operations over the past two decades.

Cloud media workflows have also seen an increasing usage in artificial intelligence (AI) and machine learning (ML). File-based workflows are enhanced with automatic metadata tagging and enrichment from speaker and object recognition, captions and keywords to language translation and recognition of onscreen text to find appropriate places for downstream promotional graphics insertion. Big data drives search optimization, audience and social media analytics, and targeted ad insertion. The viewer experience is enhanced through content personalization, curation, and accurate recommendation engines. Captions and subtitles are synchronized, and multi-language versions are generated. Even marketing is enhanced by AI with automated graphics generation. News organizations use AI to detect deepfakes. The massive compute capabilities of the cloud are enabling workflows only dreamed about just a decade ago.

Yet at the end of the last decade there were still major hurdles to cloud migration. The first rule of cloud migration should be that migration should encompass an end-to-end workflow, as every time content has to leave and return to the cloud introduces cost and latency. Cloud-based editing was still nascent, mostly a do-it-yourself affair using some flavor of remote desktop, and tools for live production in the cloud were practically non-existent save for a few web streaming tools like OBS and vMix, again as DIY implementations in the cloud.

Along comes 2020, a new decade, a new pathogen and our entire world was turned upside down. What COVID meant for most media companies in 2020 was surviving and staying on the air. Moving to the cloud added a layer of risk in world already overwhelmed with uncertainty. Yet deep down, every organization knew that the trauma of 2020 would only accelerate their cloud migration journey once they got back on their feet.

For those who had already made the journey before COVID, their ability to execute during the pandemic exemplified the value in operating from inside the cloud. New OTT platforms were launched. New ways for doing production and operations with a remote workforce became the norm. New cloud-native editing systems were launched. Cloud-based production workflows were stood up using NDI, vMix and OBS, and by the end of the year new live productions solutions from established players emerged. For many media companies, clearly the cloud is ready for media.

One of the core values of the cloud is the friction it removes that impedes collaboration with suppliers, partners and distributors. For example, recently competitors Discovery and A+E Networks, both fully operational in the cloud, collaborated on a new business endeavor and launched an OTT service without anyone going inside a single facility. They conformed, processed and shared an entire library of content in under 24 hours. The entire cost of the media collaboration processing in the cloud was around $11,000. If nothing else, 2020 was the year that proved the statement that running in the cloud was simply running your software on someone else's computer was a fallacy.

## Is The Cloud There Yet?

*Is the cloud truly there yet for media?* Yes, for almost all applications and workflows.

The cloud is now able to do live production. JPEG-XS and AWS' CDI enable low-latency live cloud workflows and 5G edge nodes offer tantalizing possibilities. New solutions emerge every day that expand the capabilities of live in the cloud but building and orchestrating live workflows is still complicated and limited. We're unlikely to see the PGA or Super Bowl mixed in the cloud anytime soon because of limited processing, scale and latency; we haven't yet developed the technology to build massive live production engines running as parallel processes across multiple cloud instances.

*Are media organizations truly ready for the cloud?* Yes, for the early adopters and cloud-native media companies.

Too many cloud systems are still maintaining legacy workflows and technologies coupled with operational silos. These lift and shift implementations not only cost too much to operate, they also fail to realize the amazing benefits the cloud can bring to media operations.

At the same time, media companies haven't fully adapted to the new cloud paradigm of on-demand capability and consumption-based costs to change their cloud economics. The best cloud-native media workflow systems can manage costs, shifting workloads to regions and times of day when its most cost effective and practical. They're able to track costs by users and customers, driving more efficient operations. Yet the media companies using these systems haven't embraced these capabilities. It's still engineering deploying systems in the cloud but lacking the ability or authority to influence the creative side. For a long time, media engineering has been a silo that serves the content side. With the cloud, it's time for a closer collaboration between content and engineering to implement optimized operations. Yet this can only happen if the leadership realizes the value in breaking down this silo as well.

## The Future of Media in The Cloud

What does the future hold for media in the cloud? What will it look like when we truly understand and leverage the cost structure of the cloud to build dynamic on-demand systems that fully utilize the massive compute, storage and bandwidth capabilities of the cloud to economically create new consumer experiences never before possible? When we break down workflow silos across not just production, playout and distribution but also creative, engineering and business units? When we totally rethink how we create media, leaving behind our legacy technologies and workflows and embrace IT and the cloud as the currency of media?

This isn't just a technology shift, it's a fundamental change in how we create and deliver media as a business. Underpinning this is a transformational cultural shift at every level, one that media companies are still in the early stages of adopting. Before we can begin that journey, we must first be willing to discard the technology and workflows of yesterday and be open to rethinking completely what it is we are trying to do. Below are two examples of the future of media in the cloud, one imminent and one perhaps not far away, that illustrate how we can leverage everything the cloud has to offer once we fully understand the cloud and leave past constraints behind.

## Cloud Future Example 1: Serverless Playout in The Cloud

Today most cloud playout systems are lift and shift transformations of legacy playout engines. The broadcast industry started the migration from purpose-built hardware and discrete playout with numerous physical components – servers, router, master control switcher, graphics, processing modules – to a software-based playout a little over a decade ago. The common design was a "channel-in-a-box" (CiaB), a single software application that ran on a single server and provided all of the functionality needed for a playout channel. In the dedicated hardware model, this design provided the scalability and resiliency media customers sought. As a fully software-based solution, it was also relatively simple to migrate to virtual machine environments and the cloud.

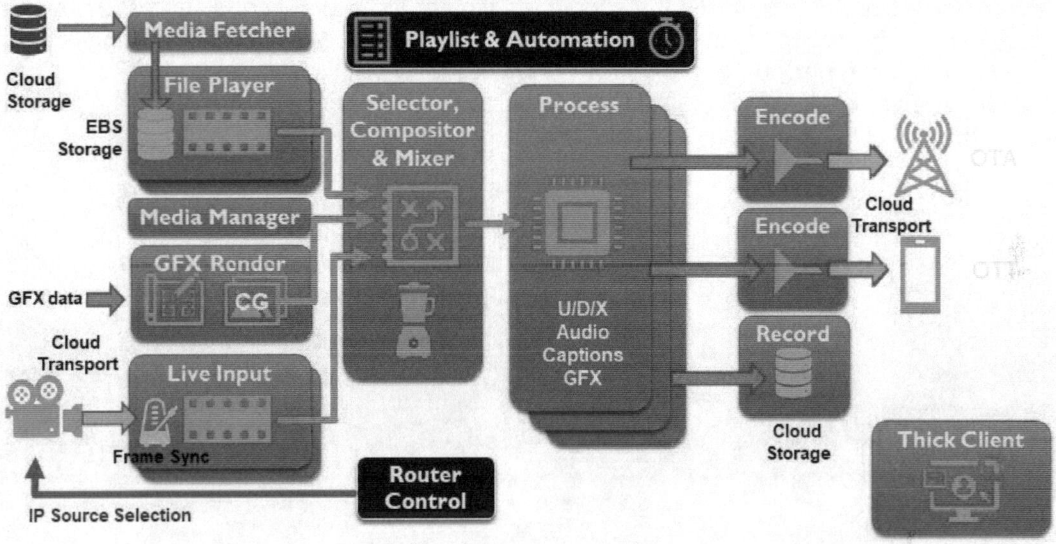


FIGURE 1: TRADITIONAL 'CHANNEL-IN-A-BOX" IT-BASED PLAYOUT ENGINE

But CiaB is exactly the wrong design for the cloud. Only a small part of what runs in the CiaB server is actually doing real-time playout and stream generation. The rest is there to perform background and itinerant tasks like media management or create the occasional graphical element in the program. In a dedicated hardware system, the CPU utilization might be 30% to leave room for simultaneous bursts of activity. In the cloud, even lower utilization is needed to protect from unknown applications running in adjacent VMs. GPUs are often required, making the cloud costs even higher. Some suppliers even require running on bare-metal instances to protect against neighboring VM applications, further increasing costs.

Cloud-native and cloud-optimized playout refactors the CiaB design, moving everything out of the playout instance that isn't needed for real-time delivery. Graphics are pre-rendered in an on-demand render grid or by using a service like Singular.live where the on-air rendering is simply an HTML5 rendering engine. Media management moves to serverless workflows driven by triggers. What was once a monolithic architecture is now several microservices each running optimized in the appropriate cloud environment. Yet this is still playout as we know it delivered by a realtime, linear processing engine, an engine that still runs at a fraction of CPU utilization in order to deliver a precisely timed transport stream output.

For most linear channels, most of the schedule if not all of it is simply playing out files back-to-back with occasional graphics overlays. What if this could be moved to a non-realtime process? As soon as a playlist was published, the playout engine would pre-render the entire playlist. In doing so, it could run the CPU at 100% without concern as the output would be to file with no need to create a precisely timed transport stream. The file could be QC'd ahead of air, providing additional confidence while eliminating the need for the backup playout server. Graphics could be rendered by CPU instead of GPU; if it slowed down the rendering process it would not matter. When content repeats in the overnight as is often the case on some channels, instead of re-rendering, only an additional manifest needs to be created, saving even more. By moving to a pre-rendered playout model based on internet technologies such as HLS, we're able to reduce cloud operating costs by 95% while increasing reliability and creating new workflow and distribution possibilities.

To make this work, the file-based output would be HLS chunks and manifest files with timing that corresponds to the scheduled airtime. At the scheduled time of air, playout consists of the downstream receiver or player simply requesting the HLS file chunks from the cloud file server. Nothing is actually running in the cloud during playout! At the edge – whether that's a cable headend or a TV station, the HLS chunks are turned into a transport stream by the IRD, a simple process. For OTT, the HLS chunks are played by the device player.

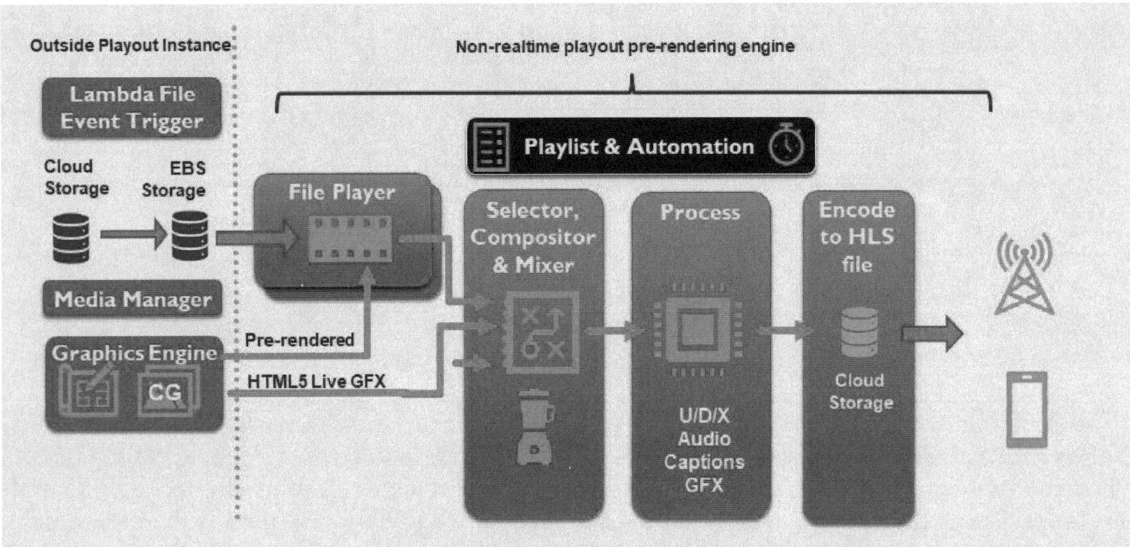


FIGURE 2: NON-REALTIME PRE-RENDERED PLAYOUT ENGINE

In this model, the actual cost to run this is around 5% of what a traditional lift and shift playout system would cost that used GPU-enabled instances with 1+1 redundancy. Yet this model provides greater resiliency – cloud storage is multiple 9s more reliable than a cloud server – and the ability to preview the content and correct errors in a playlist prior to air. The latency of this model versus the traditional model needs only to be a few seconds more depending on the HLS chunk length chosen, and part of this additional latency is offset by no longer needing ARQ protection for the delivery.

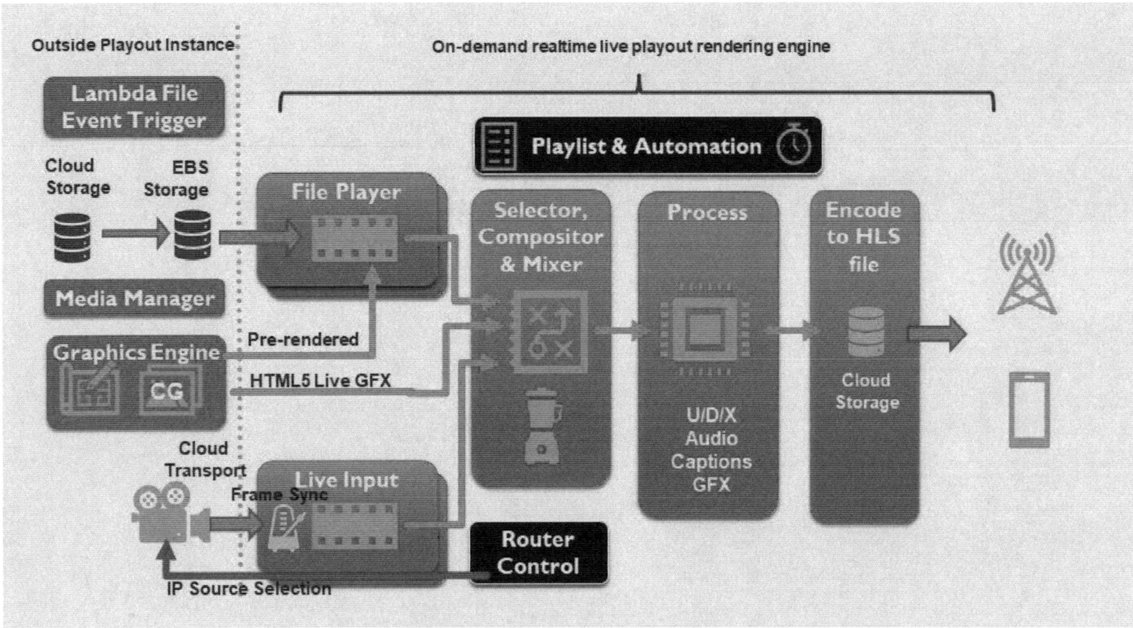


FIGURE 3: LIVE EVENT PROCESSING IN PRE-RENDERED PLAYOUT

Moving from a transport stream to an HLS file delivery model for playout provides more than simple costs savings. Live event handling is simply the process of spinning up an on-demand playout instance in realtime mode and replacing the previously recorded HLS chunks as shown below.

Unanticipated schedule delays can be accomplished by simply changing the metadata in the manifests. Different chunks can be created for each recipient, simplifying targeted ad insertion and content replacement for every affiliate or consumer. Imagine a network that delivered a unique stream to every station without standing up a separate playout engine for each. The exact same process that creates the file-based playout and live to air can be used for file to VOD and live to VOD creation unifying these workflows; the only change is in the manifest that defines an airtime for playout.

In summary, by discarding the need for transport stream outputs on playout and the recognition that most playout is actually scheduled and can be rendered far ahead of airtime we're able to create a new model for cloud playout that dramatically reduces costs while significantly improving capabilities and scalability.

## Cloud Future Example 2: Volumetric Point Cloud Live Sports Production

The past decade has seen several advancements in remote live production and remote integration (REMI) production where camera signals are home run from an event venue back to a centralized production facility across town or across the world. In most cases the remote production facility is in region to manage latency and save on bandwidth and transport costs, yet even some Olympic events have been remote produced by NBC as far back as the 2006 games in Turin.

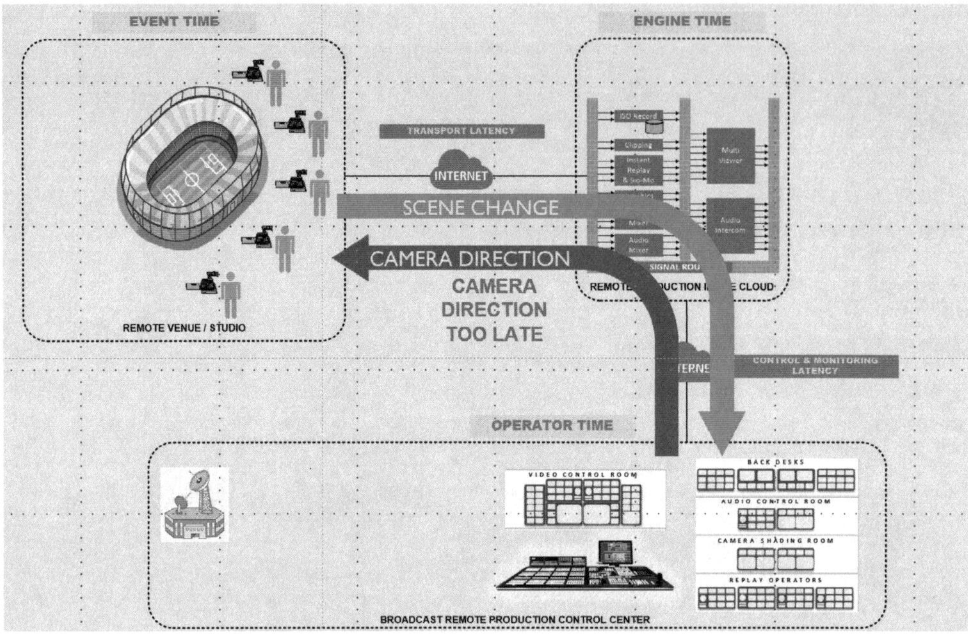


FIGURE 4: TRADITIONAL REMI AND CLOUD LIVE PRODUCTION

Moving remote production to the cloud would seem the logical next step. The cloud would let you instantiate production facilities on demand. As most production facilities are only used a fraction of the time this would result in significant savings. Production requirements and complexity vary widely from event to event, but physical production facilities have static capabilities; cloud-based systems could be orchestrated and scaled to meet the exact needs of each event.

There are several obstacles to live production in the cloud:

- **Latency** – When switching a live sports event, latency is critical. A technical director typically demands latency under 250ms from camera to control room display, and under 100ms is preferred. To achieve this, low-latency transport solutions such as JPEG-XS with sub-frame encoding have been developed, and one cloud now supports uncompressed video. Clouds are also deploying edge nodes inside 5G networks to put cloud processing as close to the event as possible.
- **Scale** – Simple production with a handful of camera feeds is doable in the cloud today, and several recently developed integrated live production systems for the cloud give users the tools and workflows they need for these events. But these systems are constrained by the number of signals and processing they can handle in a single cloud compute instance, impairing their ability to scale up for larger events and significantly limiting their capacity for UHD production. Scale requires the ability to scale live workflow processing across multiple cloud instances with parallel processing.
- **Bandwidth** – For a handful of HD cameras with JPEG-XS or NDI encoding the cloud is viable, especially when you consider that ingress bandwidth is not charged for consumption unlike egress bandwidth. That ingress is essentially free making the cloud ideal for live production where there are usually far more input signals tan outputs. Today professional sports stadiums often have 100G internet connections which would support dozens of UHD cameras with compression.

The drawing below illustrates one of the obstacles to live production in the cloud. In this example, the traditional REMI model is moved to the cloud with camera operators in the stadium feeding the cloud which then feeds the remote director. The double-hop latency between the event site and the technical director can often add more latency than is tolerable in fast-action sporting events.

The obstacles above are focused on migrating tradition live production workflows to the cloud. What if we removed "traditional" from this equation? The greatest obstacle is latency; the time from camera lens to the director's eye. What if we move the cameras and their operators into the cloud as well to eliminate that latency? What if we used latency to our advantage in live production?

The past few years have seen significant advancements in lightfield cameras and volumetric camera arrays. These use a large number of fixed cameras to capture a volume of space such as a sports playing field, and then through processing derive any desired camera angle. Examples of these are Canon's Free Viewpoint and Intel's True View technologies. Both of these have been used in live sports events to provide immersive instant replays with camera moves that bring an event to life but would be impossible with an operator-run camera.

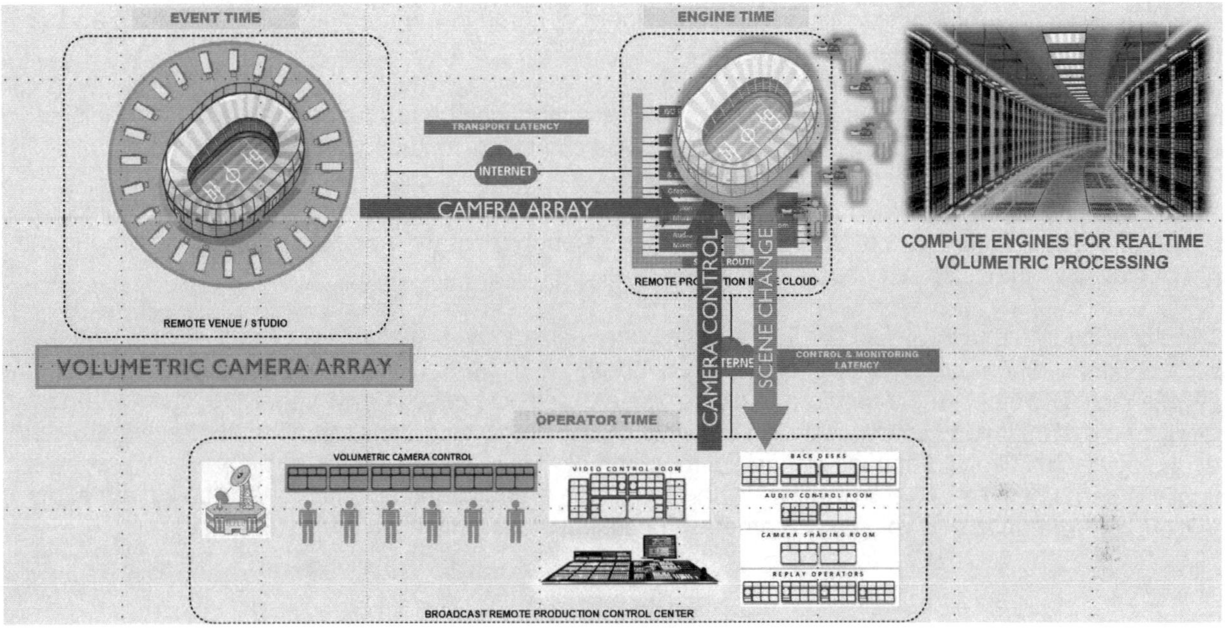


FIGURE 5: CLOUD LIVE PRODUCTION USING VOLUMETRIC CAMERAS AND ESPORTS ENGINE

In these volumetric camera applications, both are used as effects and not as realtime game coverage. The compute processing required takes considerable time as well as programming the desired move into the system. But the only difference between long render times and realtime rendering is compute capability, and this is where the cloud excels. In the cloud one can literally instantiate a supercomputer on demand as a mammoth array of instances.

Creating a volumetric point cloud representation of a playing field in realtime will require significant research and development to scale this parallel workflow across all the instances needed to render the 3D "holodeck" representation. Each camera needs to be interpolated with every other camera to provide additional resolution and virtual camera positions. The author's preliminary calculation examined a playing filed covered by 32 UHD (2160p) cameras to create the point cloud. For each camera, one CPU core received and decoded the JPEG XS feed and created a quad HD output. From there, each HD output required additional core for every other HD output in the array to create the point cloud. While the first camera only needs 4 such cores and the second camera 12 cores, the 32$^{nd}$

camera would require 496 additional cores for processing. In total, an array of 32 cameras requires 7936 cores, certainly approaching the concept of a supercomputer.

For processing efficiency, each of these compute instances is GPU enabled. In Amazon AWS, the largest and most powerful GPU instance the author found was a G4dn.metal instance, a bare-metal server with 384 GB or RAM and 96 CPU cores which cost $ 7.824/hour to run on-demand (list) or $0.0815 per core per hour. The total cost to run this system in the cloud is $646.78/hour. To put that in perspective, that's less than the cost of the diesel fuel to transport a single live production trailer to the event site. It's less that the travel and expenses for a single camera operator onsite.

The volumetric point cloud creates a realtime 3D representation of the playing field in the cloud. To then "cover" this virtual playing filed, virtual cameras are used to create any perspective desired. These are essentially identical to the concept of observer cameras in live production of esports events. The control surface for the camera operator is a gaming console controller; every esports gamer is now a potential operator for this virtual volumetric live production. Creating each virtual camera output only requires a few more cores for processing. This allows subscribers at home to run their own virtual camera and enables the system to drive immersive headsets.

With volumetric point cloud live sports production, live events can be produced that are as engaging and immersive as esports. Camera angles and moves can follow the action in a way that no human-held or sky-crane camera could. By running in the cloud with virtual cameras, the logical next step would be to add AI-enhancement to the camera moves, automatically following the ball or selected players. Replays would take on an entirely new dimension, with virtual cameras able to spin around the foot of player as they step out of bounds to show every angle.

There is of course much work to be done before such technology is available for major events. Even with the massive compute capability of the cloud today, the network I/O for these instances still remains a bottleneck. Development is required to divide these processes in such a way that they can be run in parallel across this many cores within the current I/O and processing constraints. In all likelihood, such technology is first likely to appear at more intimate events such as gymnastics and boxing where fewer cameras can be utilized, later migrating upwards through arena events such as basketball to stadiums as cloud performance and volumetric camera processing algorithms continue to advance.

## Conclusion

Cloud advancements will continue to outpace what is possible in on-premises and dedicated hardware. As technology and media companies better understand the cloud and begin to adopt cloud-native practices, new workflow models will create opportunity through better economics and utilization of the vast compute performance capabilities of the cloud.

Today we're deploying servers with 400G of connectivity or more and 96 cores of processing and a terabyte of RAM. We're able to deploy infrastructure as code, orchestrating distributed processing and workflows that scale on demand and create mammoth systems in the blink of an eye, and tear them down just as fast. Moore's law still holds true, and as long as it does, we'll soon be able to produce highly immersive live sports events in the cloud without sending a single OB vehicle or camera person to the stadium.

# Live Video Transport in the Cloud with JPEG XS and AWS CDI

**Thomas Edwards**
**Amazon Web Services**
**Santa Monica, California, United States**
tedwaa@amazon.com

**Abstract** – Media companies are used to high quality, low latency IP transport of live video using JPEG 2000 compression for WAN transport, and ST 2110-20 uncompressed video transport within the broadcast facility. However, the cloud is a very different environment - it is inherently multi-tenant, software-oriented, and achieves reliability through redundancy mechanisms that expect faults to occur. This paper discusses two new tools for live cloud video. JPEG XS is a software friendly, high quality, sub-frame latency codec to bring live video flows in to and out of cloud. The AWS Cloud Digital Interface (CDI) is a new open SDK for moving uncompressed video within the cloud. CDI is implemented on Amazon Web Services using the Scalable Reliable Datagram (SRD) protocol, which makes use of a large number of redundant paths through the cloud network to deliver reliable media transport with sub-frame latencies. JPEG XS and CDI are both being used to process live video in the cloud deployment of the new Fox Technology Center.

## Cloud Benefits and Challenges for Broadcasters

A significant trend in broadcasting is moving key workloads to the cloud, including channel ingest, video processing, content creation, archiving, and distribution operations. The faster content can be moved to the cloud, the faster that content value can be multiplied through distribution to on-cloud partners, via enhanced monetization with ad tech, and with insights from deep AI analysis. Cloud also lends itself naturally to remote production with a globalizing workforce. And cloud enables broadcasters to be able to experiment with business reinvention more freely, as cloud resources can be created or destroyed in an agile fashion to "fail fast" (or better yet "succeed fast") on new services such as personalized camera angles, novel digital viewing experiences with real-time data and augmented reality (such as LA Clippers CourtVision [1]), or fantasy sports-oriented viewing.

The supply chain for pre-recorded video content is now widely implemented in the cloud, including editing, asset management, and video compression. Live is a greater challenge, of course. Live requires never dropping a frame, and ensuring every frame is delivered on every tick of the timecode clock.

Many large broadcast facilities and OB trucks have realized tremendous efficiency in their video routing systems by moving from SDI to IP using ST 2110 over a highly managed on-premises network, timed within tens of nanoseconds by Precision Time Protocol (PTP). In some cases, software-based video processing solutions are beginning to replace hardware-based solutions, a task also made easier by the transition from SDI to IP.

This paper is excerpted from the Proceedings of the 2021 NAB Broadcast Engineering and Information Technology (BEIT) Conference, © 2021, National Association of Broadcasters, 1 M Street S.E., Washington, DC 20003 USA.

However, the cloud is a very different environment than on-premises. Networking on the cloud is shared between multiple tenants. Generally cloud networks use high-radix Clos topologies [2], shown in abstract form in Figure 1. “High-radix” means a high number of port connections to adjacent switches in the network, and Clos topologies are designed to be non-blocking. There are inherently no guarantees about end-to-end bandwidth through cloud networks, however there is a tremendous amount of bisection bandwidth available in these networks.

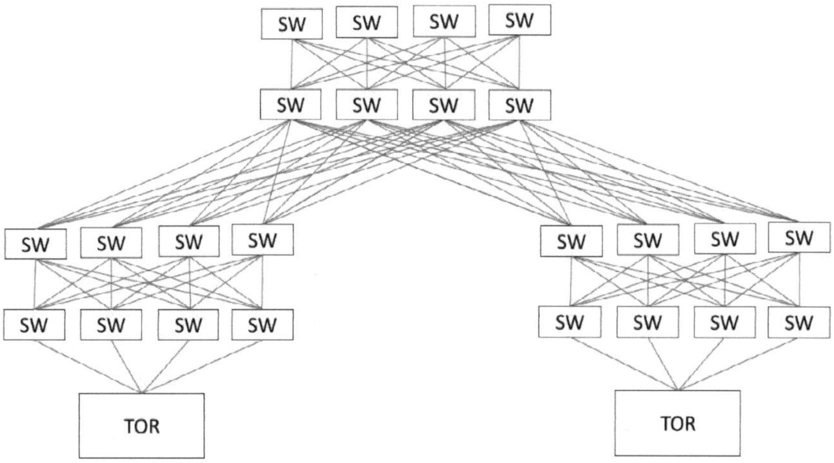


FIGURE 1: ABSTRACT EXAMPLE OF HIGH-RADIX FOLDED-CLOS NETWORK ARCHITECTURE. SW=SWITCH, TOR=TOP OF RACK SWITCH.

Also in cloud networks, it is expected that there will be link failures, switch failures, occasional congestion, and occasional switch downtime for maintenance or upgrades. But the overall network architecture is resilient and is expected to continue to operate despite these events. This is in stark contrast to on-premises low-radix or star networks where failure events in a “primary” network may require a failover to a “secondary” network, and in some situations two or more failures may lead to blocked signal paths.

Cloud networks usually use the equal-cost multipath (ECMP) routing strategy where next-hop packet forwarding to a destination could occur over one of many possible paths. The path through the network taken by a particular flow depends on the IP 5-tuple (source IP, destination IP, protocol number, source port, and destination port), as illustrated in Figure 2. Switches hash the 5-tuple to decide which output port of the switch is used to send the packet to the next hop. Across a large population of different flows, ECMP helps to spread them out across multiple paths to efficiently make use of the full bisection bandwidth of the mesh of paths from source to destination. Also, a failure event in a small portion of the mesh can be routed around while maintaining end-to-end connectivity.

ST 2110 IP video flows are what network engineers call “elephant flows” due to their large size (1 Gbit/s or more). In an ECMP network, when the hash values of two (or more) elephant flows collide, they have to share the same link with reduced throughput even though other paths may be completely free. On-premises broadcast networks require careful network management to avoid such collisions, sometimes using software defined networking technology (for example, see [3]). Or the networks can be built in a “star topology” using a single large modular switch, some of which can deliver port counts as high as 2304 x 10G Ethernet ports [4].

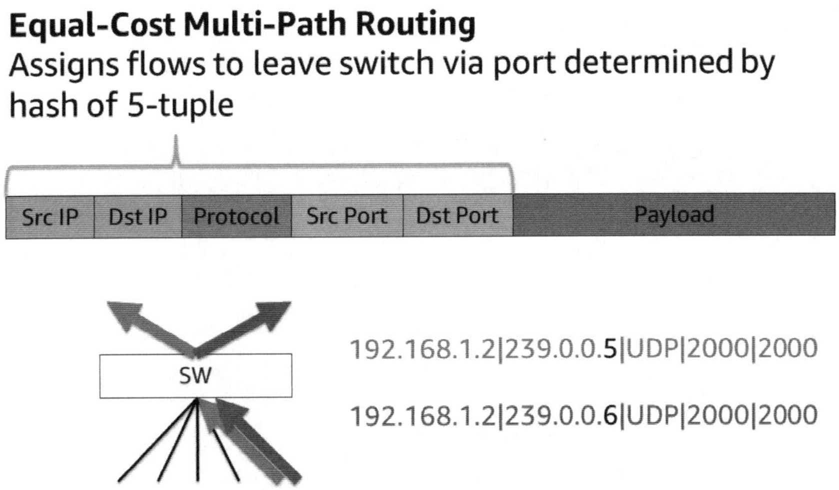


FIGURE 2: ECMP AND THE IP 5-TUPLE

## Scalable Reliable Datagram Protocol

Amazon Web Services developed the Scalable Reliable Datagram (SRD) protocol [5] initially to address use cases in high performance computing. SRD is optimized for hyper-scale datacenters. It provides load balancing across multiple paths and fast recovery from packet drops or link failures. It utilizes standard ECMP functionality on commodity Ethernet switches and works around its limitations. SRD employs a specialized congestion control algorithm that helps further decrease the chance of packet drops and minimizes retransmit times.

SRD is implemented on the AWS Nitro System [6] that that offloads and accelerates IO for functions, increasing overall virtual server instance system performance. SRD is exposed to the host as an Elastic Fabric Adapter (EFA) PCIe device. EFA has a custom-built operating system bypass hardware interface to enhance the performance of inter-instance communications, reducing latency, jitter, avoiding OS system calls, and reducing memory copies. This allows applications to perform high levels of inter-node communications at scale.

The SRD sender "sprays" packets of a single application flow across multiple simultaneous network paths to minimize the chance of hotspots and to detect failed or suboptimal paths. The number of different paths can be on the order of 32. The sender controls the ECMP path selection by manipulating packet encapsulation. Round trip time (RTT) is calculated on each path to detect increasing congestion or failure along the path. Congestion can be routed around on other paths, and failure leading to packet loss is healed by retransmitting the packet on a working path. Because each path represents only a fraction of the entire flow, a single failure results in a small packet loss that is rapidly retransmitted.

SRD is thus able to deliver reliable transport of flows over an existing cloud network, while sharing the network with legacy traffic. Figure 3 shows that SRD is able to maintain far more consistent bandwidth than plain UDP for multiple flows across a cloud network. Figure 4 shows that SRD recovers far more rapidly from a network link impairment than UDP since packets can be immediately shifted to other paths without waiting for routing reconvergence. No significant network device upgrades are required for SRD implementation. The existing ECMP routing remains unchanged, only endpoint interfaces need to be aware of the protocol.

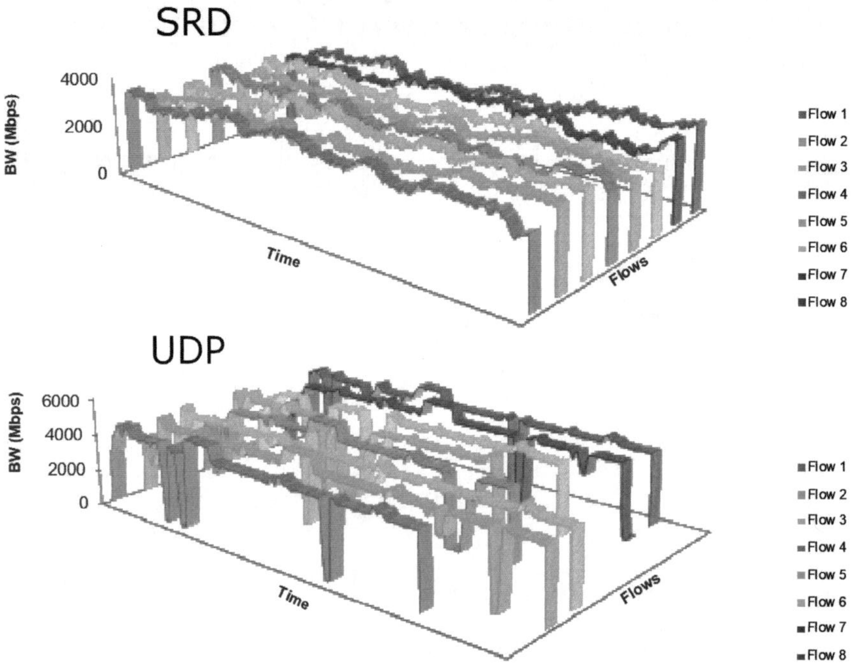


FIGURE 3: BANDWIDTH RELIABILITY OF SRD VS. UDP IN A CLOUD NETWORK

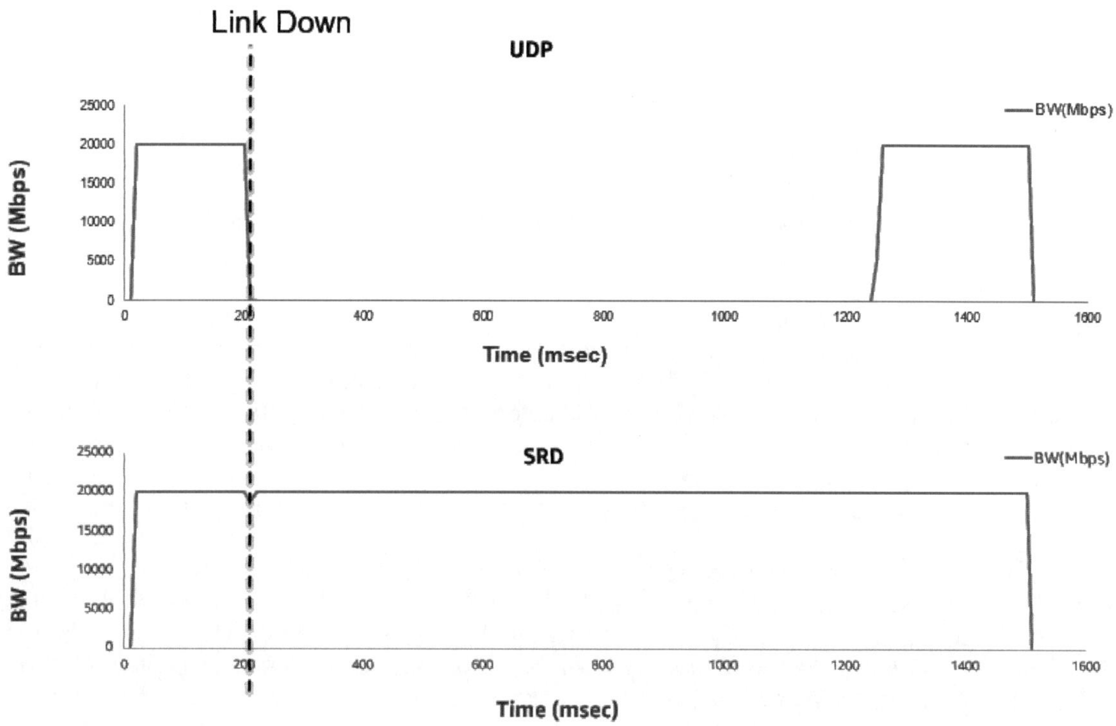


FIGURE 4: RAPID RECOVERY FROM NETWORK LINK IMPAIRMENT IN SRD VS. UDP

## AWS Cloud Digital Interface SDK

The AWS Cloud Digital Interface (CDI) SDK is the library which implements the low-latency reliable transport of data between systems in the cloud including AWS Media Services and Amazon Elastic Compute Cloud (EC2) virtual server instances. It uses SRD to send uncompressed video with network latency as low as a single frame of video between the sending and receiving applications.

The AWS CDI SDK provides an Audio/Video/Metadata (AVM) API to send video data between instances, and a RAW API to send generic data. The AVM API allows you to easily map SMPTE ST 2110 streams to the CDI for transport. CDI AVM video uses the same pixel group ("pgroup") sample layout as ST 2110-20. But unlike ST 2110-20, CDI also allows for a video alpha channel. CDI AVM audio payloads follow the formatting of ST 2110-30, and similarly Ancillary Data payloads follow the formatting of ST 2110-40.

The AWS CDI SDK is available on GitHub [7] and is open source licensed under the BSD-2-Clause license [8].

To move the needle forward on CDI implementation, AWS hosted a two-day virtual AWS CDI Interoperability Workshop in June 2021, which resulted in more than 100 new CDI integrations between 13 ISV participants as well as AWS Media Services.

## JPEG XS and ST 2110-22

AWS CDI is used for transporting the highest-quality, uncompressed media with the lowest latency between virtual server instances in a single Availability Zone (AZ), which is one or more discrete data centers with redundant power, networking, and connectivity in an AWS Region. To move media between on-premises and the cloud, or between AZs, mezzanine compression is required. JPEG XS is a very promising codec for these use cases.

JPEG XS is standardized as ISO/IEC 21122. It is not directly related to the JPEG that uses DCT commonly used on the Internet, nor is it directly related to JPEG 2000 which is widely used for high quality, low-latency contribution encoding for broadcast. It is a unique codec developed to deliver coding efficiency similar to that of JPEG 2000, but with sub-frame latency and using algorithms that can be readily implemented in software. The design goal of JPEG XS was to have a complexity such that 4K 60p video could be encoded on an Intel Core i7 processor in real time. In comparison, JPEG 2000 is considered impractical for software implementations of real-time encoding. JPEG 2000 is also generally implemented as a "full-frame" codec, resulting in latencies of 2 or more frames. In comparison, JPEG XS can have end-to-end latency as low as 32 lines of video.

To ensure the codec was visually lossless, JPEG XS was put through a rigorous subjective quality assessment during its development [9], following recommendations found in ISO/IEC 29170-2 (AIC Part-2) Draft Amendment 2 [10]. For this test, the screen is split in two parts. On one side, the original still image is displayed. On the other side, the encoded-decoded image is displayed, interleaved periodically with the original image. Both the encoded-decoded image and the original appear four times per second on the interleaved side. Any visually perceptible discrepancies between the original image and the encoded-decoded image appear as "flickering". The subjects are required to guess on which side of the screen the interleaved content is displayed.

JPEG XS has very low multi-generation loss, less than 1 dB PSNR-Y' over 10 coding/decoding cycles. In comparison with JPEG 2000 "full frame" encoding, JPEG XS has comparable PSNR-Y' encoding quality at the cost of about 20%-35% additional data rate [11]. Our customers have been using JPEG XS at 5:1 to 10:1 compression levels (110-220 Mbps for 720p59.94 format, for example).

JPEG XS can be transported over IP as per SMPTE ST 2110-22 "Professional Media Over Managed IP Networks: Constant Bit-Rate Compressed Video", which specifies the RTP transport of constant bitrate compressed video in ST 2110 systems. The RTP payload for JPEG XS is defined by IETF draft-lugan-payload-rtp-jpegxs, expected to shortly become published as an RFC.

## AWS CDI & JPEG XS Cloud Workflows

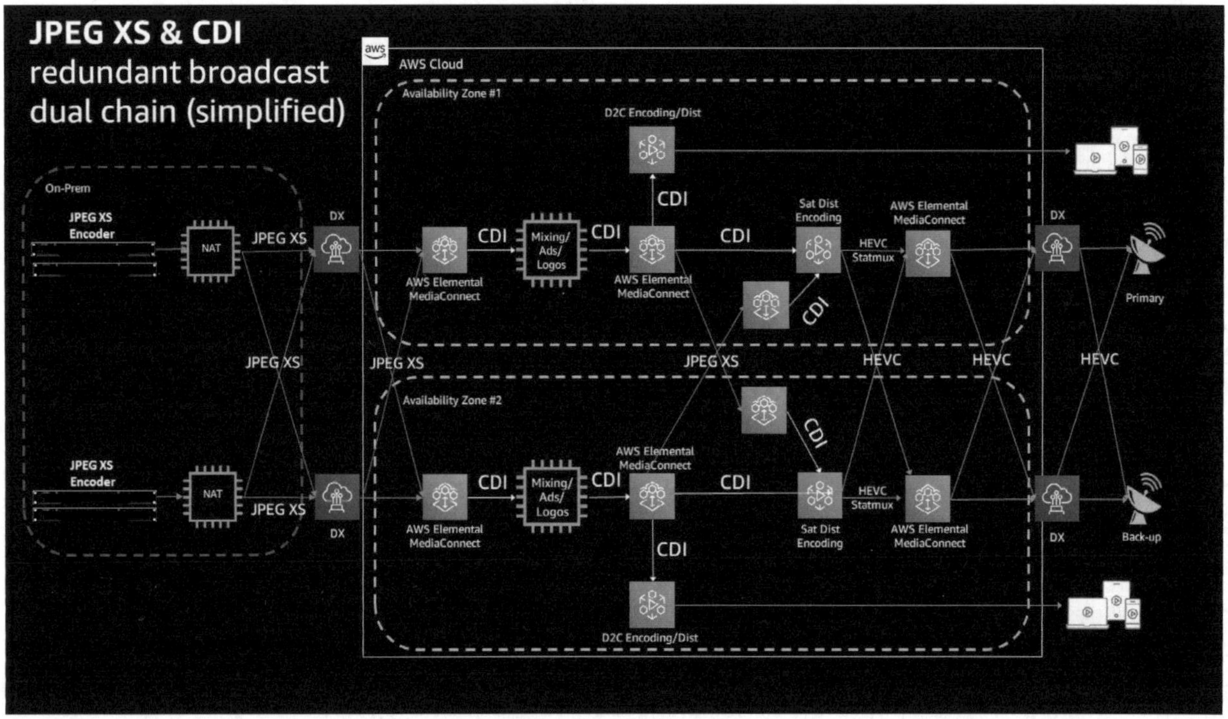


FIGURE 5: JPEG XS AND CDI REDUNDANT BROADCAST DUAL CHAIN ARCHITECTURE EXAMPLE

Figure 5 is an example of a redundant broadcast dual chain architecture which uses JPEG XS encoding to move live video onto the cloud and between AZs, uses CDI to move video between live processing steps inside an AZ, encodes output for Direct-to-Consumer (D2C) Internet distribution, and encodes an HEVC statmux for delivery to satellite uplink facilities.

JPEG XS on-premises encoders generate two redundant ST 2110-22 RTP flows which are processed by Network Address Translation (NAT) systems so that the IP flows can be properly sent over AWS Direct Connect (DX), which are low latency, secure and private connections to AWS for workloads which require higher speed or lower latency than the Internet. The redundant JPEG XS flows are delivered to AWS Elemental MediaConnect, which performs a SMPTE ST 2022-7 seamless source failover if one of the two flows experiences packet losses.

AWS Elemental MediaConnect decodes the JPEG XS sources into uncompressed CDI, which flows into video processing systems running on EC2 servers. These systems perform video switching, advertising insertion, logo and graphics insertion, multiviewers, and other typical broadcast processing functionality. CDI outputs then flow into another MediaConnect, which distributes CDI to HEVC statmux encoders (such as AWS Elemental MediaLive) as well as distributing CDI to D2C encoding and distribution. This MediaConnect also encodes the video into JPEG XS for transport to a MediaConnect running in another AZ for redundancy.

In addition, HEVC compressed outputs are sent to an egress MediaConnect both in the same AZ and also in another AZ for redundancy, and from there the HEVC flows over DX to primary and secondary satellite uplinks. This highly redundant architecture avoids any single point of failure risks.

## Conclusions

The combination of JPEG XS and CDI allow for very high-quality, low-latency live video transport for the most demanding and high-visibility cloud broadcast workflows. JPEG XS in ST 2110-22 is a standardized codec that works well in both hardware and software implementations and is an excellent tool for moving video on to and off of the cloud, as well as between cloud AZs or Regions. CDI is an open-source SDK for reliably moving uncompressed live video in a cloud AZ by taking advantage of the inherent physical structure of cloud networks. When combined together, highly effective and reliable live broadcast chains can be architected in the cloud, and customers are already beginning to build cloud broadcast solutions with these tools, such as the new Fox Technology Center [12].

## References


[1] Anderson, L., "LA Clippers take the Clippers CourtVision viewing experience to the next level with AWS", *AWS Media Blog*, Feb. 22, 2019, https://aws.amazon.com/blogs/media/la-clippers-take-the-clippers-courtvision-viewing-experience-to-the-next-level-with-aws

[2] Clos, C. "A study of non-blocking switching networks," *The Bell System Technical Journal*, vol. 32, no. 2, pp. 406-424, March 1953, doi: 10.1002/j.1538-7305.1953.tb01433.x.

[3] Sneddon, S., Swisher, C. and Mayzurk, J., "Large Scale Deployment of SMPTE 2110: The IP Live Production Facility," *SMPTE Annual Technical Conference 2019*, pp. 1-31, doi: 10.5594/M001886.

[4] Arista Networks, "Arista 7500R Series Data Center Switch Router Data Sheet", https://www.arista.com/assets/data/pdf/Datasheets/7500RDataSheet.pdf

[5] Shalev, L.,Ayoub, H., Bshara, N., and Sabbag, E., "A Cloud-Optimized Transport Protocol for Elastic and Scalable HPC," *IEEE Micro*, vol. 40, no. 6, pp. 67-73, 1 Nov.-Dec. 2020, doi: 10.1109/MM.2020.3016891. https://ieeexplore.ieee.org/document/9167399

[6] Amazon Web Services, "AWS Nitro System", https://aws.amazon.com/ec2/nitro/

[7] Amazon Web Services, "AWS CDI SDK", https://github.com/aws/aws-cdi-sdk

[8] Open Source Initiative, "The 2-Clause BSD License", https://opensource.org/licenses/BSD-2-Clause

[9] Willème, A., Richter, T., Rosewarne, C., and Macq, B., "Overview of the JPEG XS objective evaluation procedures", *Proc. SPIE 10396, Applications of Digital Image Processing XL*, 103960N (19 September 2017); https://doi.org/10.1117/12.2273168

[10] ISO/IEC 29170-2:2015 Information technology - Advanced image coding and evaluation - Part 2: Evaluation procedure for nearly lossless coding." https://www.iso.org/standard/66094.html

[11] Edwards, T., and Smith, M., "High Throughput JPEG 2000 for Broadcast and IP-Based Applications," *SMPTE Motion Imaging Journal*, vol. 130, no. 4, pp. 22-35, May 2021, doi: 10.5594/JMI.2021.3066183.

[12] Anderson, L., "FOX: Uncompressed live sports in the cloud", *AWS Media Blog*, 19 Feb. 2021, https://aws.amazon.com/blogs/media/watch-now-fox-uncompressed-live-sports-in-the-cloud/

# Smart Compression with Artificial Intelligence

**Richard Fliam, Nelson Francisco**
**MediaKind**
**Frisco, Texas, United States**

**Abstract** – Today's media landscape must serve a broader range of media platforms and consumption models than ever before. Broadcasters and content owners require workflows that allow them to flex their offerings and create unique, personalized content offerings that can serve audiences that are continually splitting their attention between linear TV and digital content. Flexibility is important for content creation, keeping up with scale in demand, and business continuity.

A key component of any content workflow is compression. For content creators, video encoding can be the most critical part of a workflow. It ensures the content is available to an increased number of viewers and devices. Video compression can be very compute-intensive, but there is always a balance between processing power and bitrate efficiency. A key question for operators today is: how can we make the best use of the available resources while ensuring that the number of services fit into that resource pool?

This is where Artificial Intelligence (AI)-based compression technology comes into the mix. In a video encoder, AI can be used to understand the type of video content and then map the way that the encoder uses its processing options to achieve the best results. With the array of different content available, AI-based compression aims to adaptively apply all available compute resource using the most beneficial balance between the possible encoding features. This process ensures that the processing power can be spent where it is most effective for that type of content.

This session will uncover the benefits of using AI-based compression technology and the impact this leading innovation will have on the broadcast industry. Attendees will discover more about the latest algorithm developed by MediaKind's innovation team that ensures processing is used optimally and density is improved with AI-based compression.

## Decisions, Decisions – Making Them Faster

A video encoder has one mission: optimizing the video quality and bitrate. A broadcast video encoder has one more unique constraint; it must do this in real-time. A broadcast video encoder acting as a source for a 60fps live channel only has 16.6ms per frame of compute time. Good broadcast video encoders need to make the right decisions *fast*. Let's explore how we can use AI to make better decisions more quickly.

It may seem odd for those who do not build encoders to think of them as making decisions. We tend to think of programs as taking an input and producing an output with only 'if else' statements guiding the 'decisions' in the program. To understand AI's role in speeding up an encoder, we must ask: What does it *decide* between? What is the basis of that decision? And what even *is* a decision?

This paper is excerpted from the Proceedings of the 2021 NAB Broadcast Engineering and Information Technology (BEIT) Conference, © 2021, National Association of Broadcasters, 1 M Street S.E., Washington, DC 20003 USA.

## Defining a Decision

Most people are familiar with binary decisions. If our dog is good, we feed it treats. If our computer freezes, we reboot it. Should we undertake an act or not.

Something which takes an input set and returns a set of *decisions* is called a *decision function.* Decision functions may take on more forms than binary. For example, we might say if the price of a house is more than 400 dollars per square foot, we will not buy it. This forms a straight line on a graph dividing prices per square foot into 'do' and 'do not' buy. The line dividing 'do' from 'do not' buy is called a *decision boundary* and can be incredibly complex. Some example decision boundaries are pictured below.

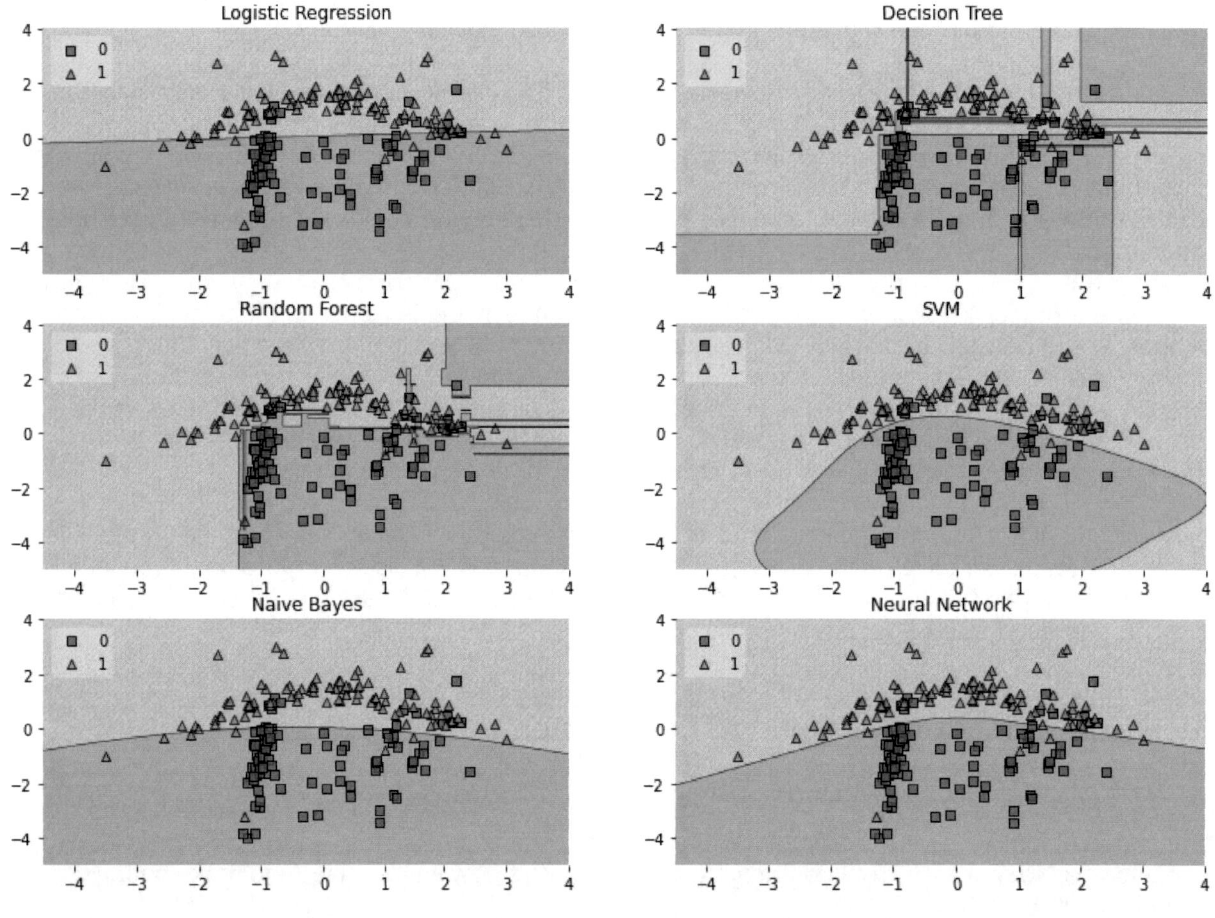


FIGURE 1: VARIOUS ALGORITHMS' DECISION BOUNDARIES [1]

A decision function can return *more* than simply 'do' or 'do not.' It may also return how likely it is that the decision is correct, generally based on how far something is from the decision boundary. This is a *statistical decision function.*

## What an Encoder Decides

So, what does an encoder decide between? Coding tools. Coding tools are options for compressing the images in a video. The choice of a particular coding tool for compression is called a "*mode.*" For example, an encoder may choose to use pixels from a different frame in the video to fill in information in a frame. Or it may choose to use pixels from the same frame but in a different location to fill in part of the frame. These are called inter (between frames) and intra (inside a frame) prediction "modes."

To make new codecs more efficient, encoders have been given more coding tools. However, with the addition of more tools, the encoder must make more decisions. In a broadcast encoder, these decisions must be made in real time. Making these decisions is more than 90% of the work an encoder does.

The primary tools available in modern codecs are a coding block tree, intra-prediction, inter-prediction, transform coding, entropy encoding, and post-processing filters. Each of these may be combined and may have dozens of possible options to use. For example, in AV1, each block of pixels may be split one of ten ways, recursively, and be predicted from neighboring blocks or other frames in dozens of ways.

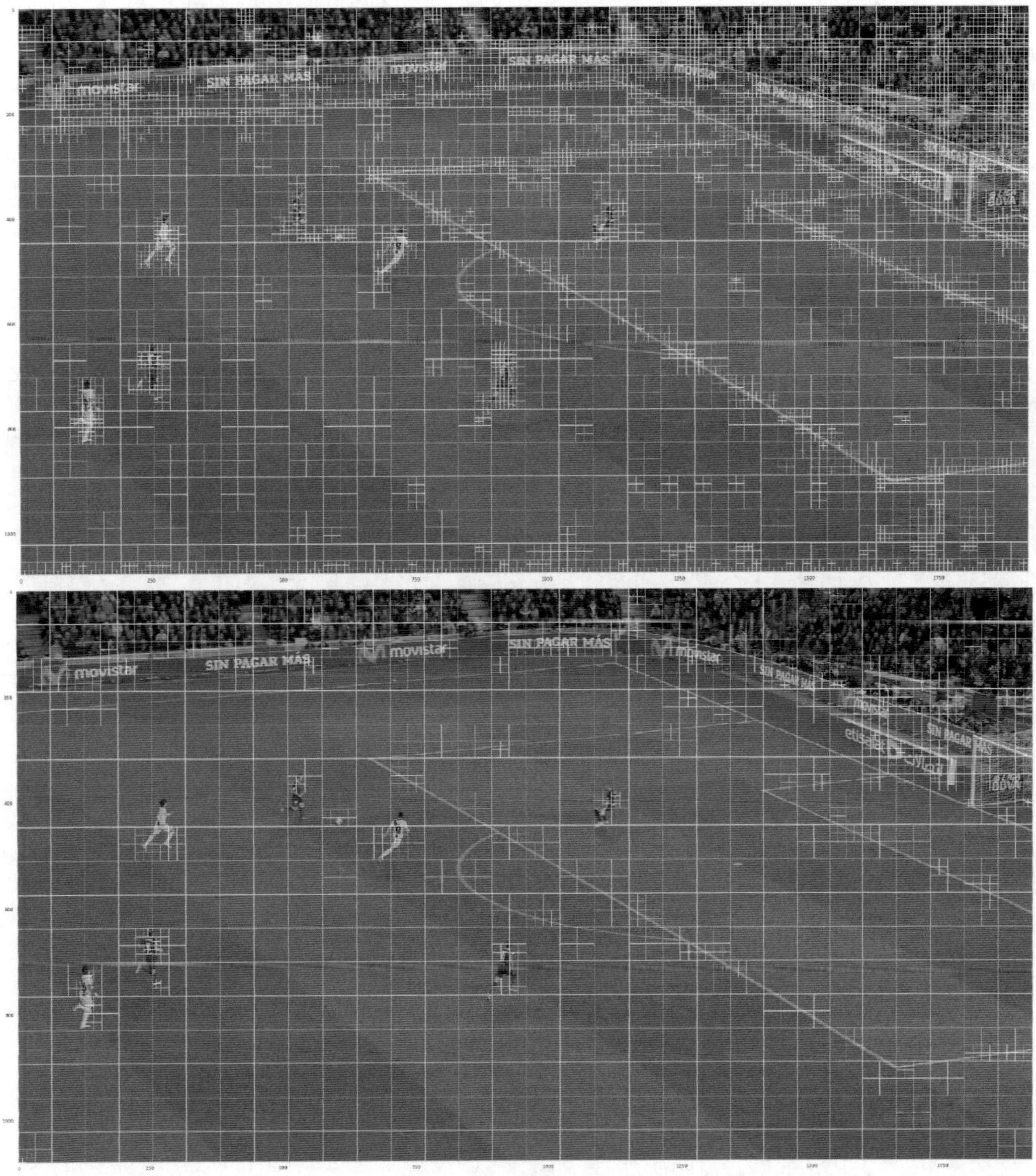


FIGURE 2: TWO OPTIONS FOR SPLITTING THE CTUS OF A VIDEO FRAME BASED ON DIFFERENT TARGET QUALITIES

## How an Encoder Decides

An encoder decides between various coding tools by looking at metrics that judge how much visual distortion is introduced using a tool and how many bits were used to produce the result. This is a process known as rate distortion optimization. An encoder will generally decide to use the tools that either give the lowest distortion for a given rate or the lowest rate for a target distortion.

## Decisions via Brute Force

The simplest method of decision making is to try all methods. If we were on a game show with prizes hidden behind doors, we could simply open all the doors and look inside and pick the best one. As the number of doors increases, we may not have time to open them before we must decide.

The option of checking all coding tools for a given frame is "exhaustive" or "full" rate distortion optimization. The encoder simply attempts to compress each block in every way possible and selects the tool which minimizes its bitrate or maximizes its picture quality.

Exhaustive rate distortion optimization is generally not possible for a broadcast encoder operating in real time. There are dependencies between decisions that make parallelism difficult or impossible to expand past a certain point. Compute in either GPU (Graphics Processing Unit) or CPU (Central Processing Unit) is simply too slow to consider all options inside a target latency budget.

## Decisions via Heuristics

To speed up this process, codec engineers implement hand-tuned heuristics. The heuristics discard comparing certain options based on mathematical models and quickly computable metrics that indicate a likelihood of success. These models effectively create a handmade decision boundary for whether to test certain coding tools. For example, Liu, et al. implement the fast CTU (Coding Tree Unit) splitting algorithm described in Figure 3 below.

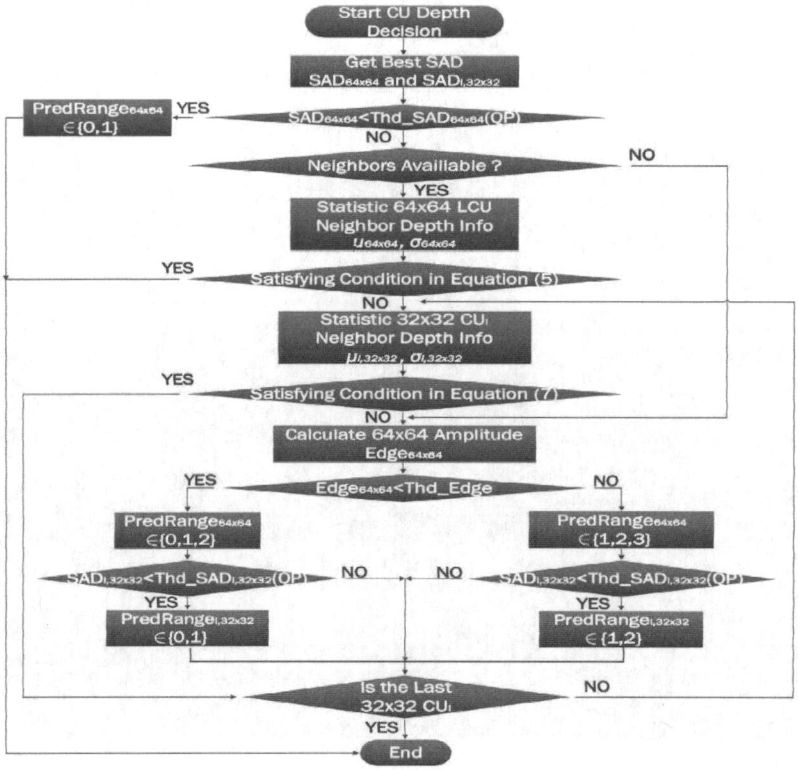


FIGURE 3: AN EXAMPLE "HAND CREATED" ALGORITHM FOR SKIPPING CERTAIN CTU DECISIONS [2]

### Decisions via Machine Learning

Rather than using hand created models to determine which modes we can use machine learning to generate the decision function, our machine models need to choose a set of input data to work off, and a set of resulting target data. The model could work directly against the image features itself or previously defined metrics. The tradeoffs are discussed in Figure 4.

| CNN | NN classifier |
| --- | --- |
| 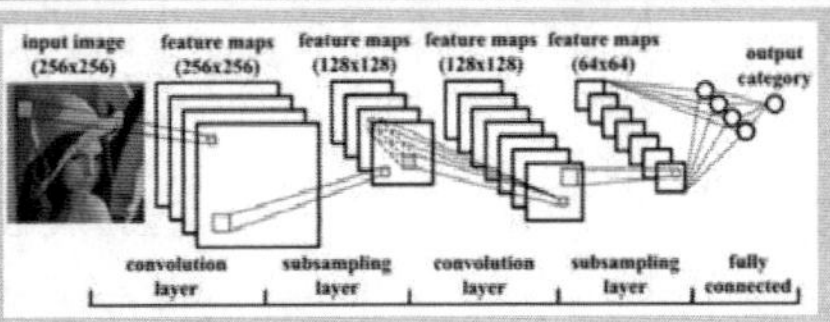 | 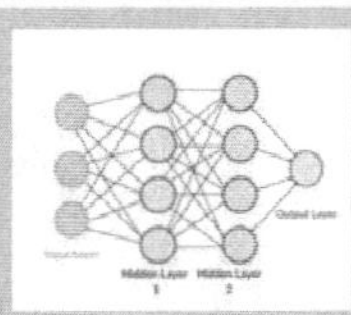 |
| • Extracts features right from the raw data.<br>• Very effective for image classification. | • Classifier can operate on existing metrics, and some of the available metrics already tackle Inter frame dependencies.<br>• Much lower complexity.<br>• Inference can be run in CPU, so no special hardware required. |
| • Higher complexity. Inference may require use of GPU for practical usage.<br>• Using a GPU may pose problems with bandwidth for memory transfers.<br>• Inter frame dependencies requires use of additional data, and its usage is not trivial. | • Relies on the correlation of the underlying metrics to achieve good accuracy.<br>• Metrics available may not be the more accurate for the classification problem. |

FIGURE 4: TRADEOFFS BETWEEN DIRECT IMAGE PROCESSING USING CNNS (CONVOLUTIONAL NEURAL NETWORKS) AND CLASSIFIER NEURAL NETWORKS

Given the compute and performance complexity of CNNs, for an encoder focused on broadcast, using quickly computable metrics and classifier algorithms is necessary. A large variety of decisions can be made using this methodology. However, all neural network models are computationally costly and may not outperform a simple hand-tuned model. As such, we focus on the most computationally intensive tools: CU (Coding Unit) Splitting and Mode prediction.

## Using AI for CU Splitting

### What is CU Splitting?

HEVC generalized H264 16x16 macroblocks into CTUs, which can be 64x64, 32x32, and 16x16 pixels in size. Each CTU can then be divided in CUs, using a quadtree splitting. CU sizes range from the CTU size down to 8x8 pixels. Prediction decision is performed individually for each CU. Each CU's cost (trade-off rate and distortion) is evaluated against the cost of splitting the CU in smaller CUs. The segmentation tree is pruned, and the optimized tree is used to represent the LCU (largest coding unit).

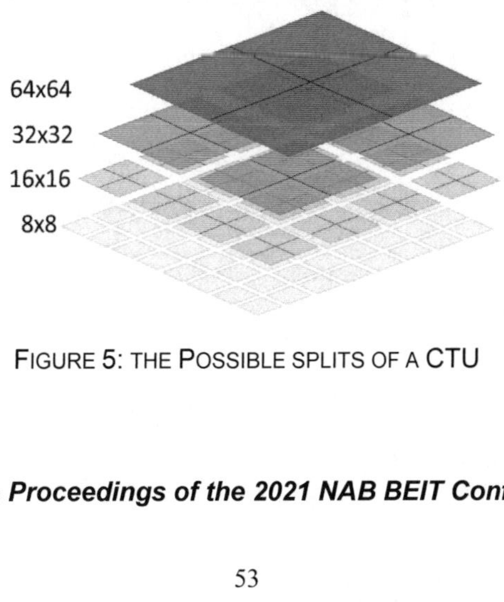


FIGURE 5: THE POSSIBLE SPLITS OF A CTU

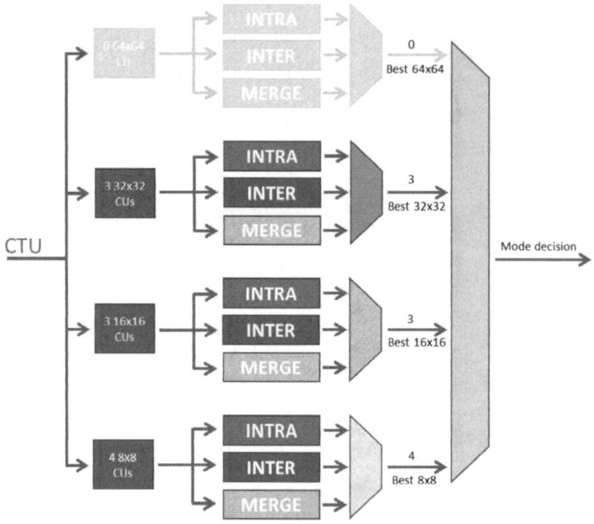


FIGURE 6: SKIPPED SPLIT DECISIONS RESULTING FROM AI

## Training the Neural Network

When training a neural network using supervised learning, 'good' data is needed. To do this, we encode many clips using long running exhaustive RDO (Rate Distortion Optimization). This spits out our input metrics of spatial activity and inter-complexity. The output was simply the set of CU splits for the frame.

The neural network infers a segmentation vector from the input spatiotemporal-complexity metric vector. The inferred vector is compared with the optimal vector flag obtained from the encoding process, and a comparison is performed using different loss functions. Backpropagation is applied, and the neural network is updated.

This process is pictured in Figure 7.

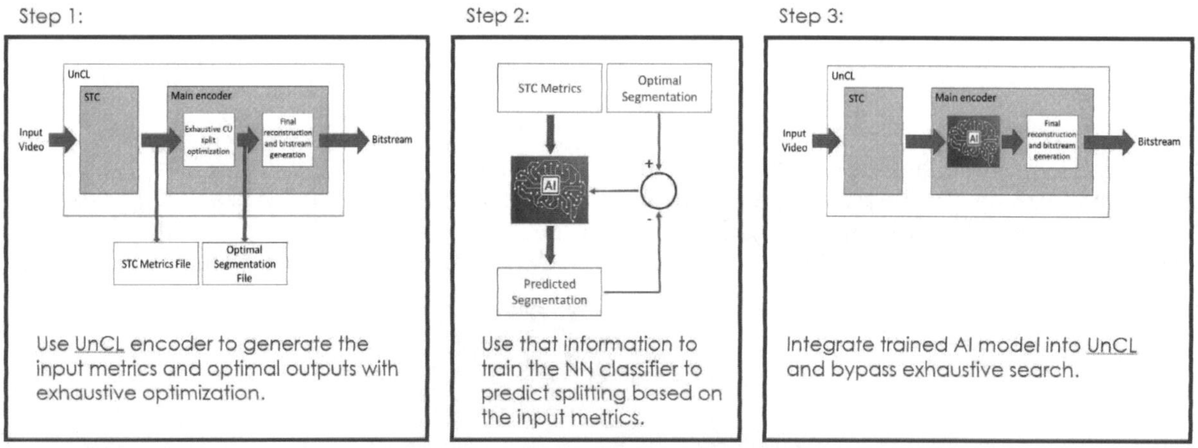


FIGURE 7: PROCESS FOR TRAINING CLASSIFIER

One of the key issues related to neural networks is interpretability. When a mis-decision is made, debugging can be difficult. However, a major advantage of using the metrics as a source for decisioning is that the inter and intra complexity metrics can be visualized to help debug and troubleshoot content that is compressed poorly.

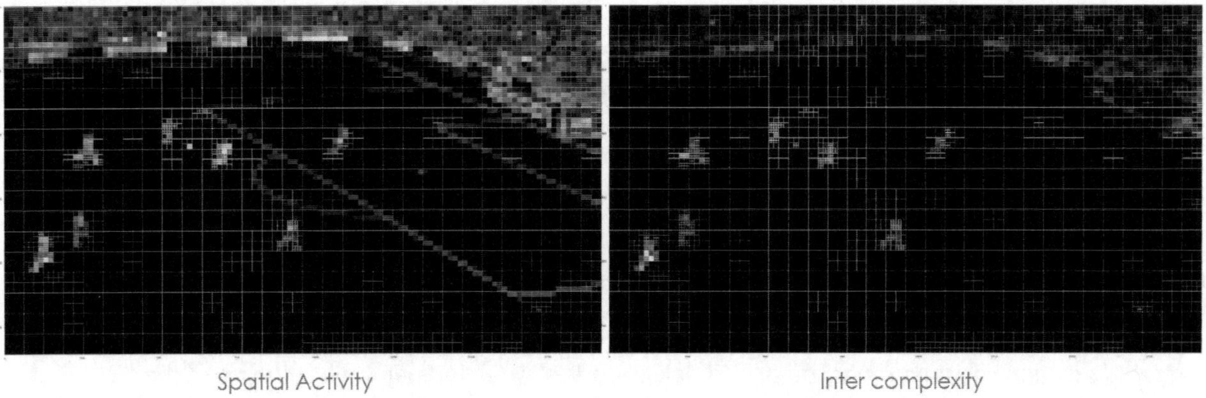


FIGURE 8: VISUALIZING COMPLEXITY METRICS

In addition, by varying network size and complexity, selectable speeds may be achieved. Denser, larger networks are slower but achieve more accuracy in coding decisions.

## Conclusion

Modern broadcast video encoders can provide significantly better picture quality at a lower bitrate by using neural network architectures to prune the set of coding tools an encoder will consider. The ability of deep learning to consider large amounts of data and fit a decision boundary to fine grained features out computes human-developed algorithms. However, deep learning is extremely compute intensive, and the cost of selecting among coding tools must be carefully weighed against the cost of checking those coding tools.

For broadcast encoders operating in real time, methods that train networks against a set of input and output metrics - rather than methods that work directly with the raw image data - are required to meet performance and latency guarantees necessary in the broadcasting world. Many encoding mode decisions can be accelerated in this manner, not just CTU splitting. Using these methods, MediaKind can achieve compression within 6% of full RDO decisioning with half the compute resources.

## References

[1] Pipis, G., "Decision Boundaries in Python," *Python in Plain English*, https://python.plainenglish.io/.

[2] Liu, J., et al., "An Adaptive Inter CU Depth Decision Algorithm for HEVC," *Visual Communications and Image Processing*, IEEE Press, Singapore, 2015.

# The Importance of Remote Access, Virtualization, and Hybrid Cloud for Live and Post Production

**Karen D. Gondoly**
**Leostream Corporation**
**Waltham, Massachusetts, United States**
kgondoly@leostream.com

**Abstract** – As virtualization and GPU technologies evolve, the Media & Entertainment industry is discovering that adopting a remote access strategy with a hybrid cloud approach is a strategic imperative. Virtualization and cloud technologies provide distinct advantages for an industry tasked with producing high-quality content in a reduced amount of time. Building a cost-effective, secure, reliable, and global solution requires organizations to ask important questions at the beginning of their infrastructure design, to ensure the success of their creative workforce. Considerations for choosing a cloud and display protocol, enabling collaboration, ensuring remote access, securing content and resources, and tracking resource usage, as described in this paper, are the key to this success.

## Introduction

There is no silver bullet, except perhaps in the movies. The technologies, use cases, and architectures you'll employ to satisfy live and post production workflows in your datacenter, on set, in the cloud, using virtualization, or in a hybrid environment depend on a number of factors. Factors that are unique to your project, your organization, and your users.

By following trends in technologies and architectures, however, you can maximize your return on investment while building a future-proofed solution that enables creatives and editors to be more productive in today's world. Today's workforce is not just mobile, but remote; initially forced to separate, but now enjoying the benefits in lifestyle and productivity that being able to work from anywhere provides.

At the heart of those technologies and architectures, lie the cloud and virtualization. Virtualization - initially deployed on-premises - started the transition away from dedicated hardware under creatives' and editors' desks. The cloud completed the journey and brought with it a number of well-documented benefits - some common across industries, but others unique to live and post production workflows.

Among the benefits of using a remote access solution for live and post production workflows are:

- Increased content security
- Elastic capacity for rapid scalability
- Access to talent outside of city centers
- Ability to react faster to client requests
- Easier on-boarding for contractors
- Support for remote users
- Easily repurposed editing rooms and workstations

This paper is excerpted from the Proceedings of the 2021 NAB Broadcast Engineering and Information Technology (BEIT) Conference, © 2021, National Association of Broadcasters, 1 M Street S.E., Washington, DC 20003 USA.

This article describes the hybrid technologies required to architect a cloud-based and virtualization-hosted remote access solution for live and post production workflows, and shares key considerations when choosing from among the available technology options. The goal is to enable your organization to reap the previously listed benefits, so you can make the movies that make the silver bullets.

The following sections share the wealth of knowledge that Leostream has gained from working with our Media & Entertainment customers as they've designed and implemented remote access solutions for their live and post production workflows. The individuals interviewed for this article prefer to remain anonymous to protect the intellectual property of their organizations. Leostream thanks them for sharing their wisdom.

## Overview of Remote Access and Cloud Technologies

A number of dedicated solutions for live and post production workflows exist on the market, such as BeBop and AWS Nimble Studio.[1] Note, however, that these solutions are not the focus of this discussion. Dedicated solutions provide quick and simplified methods for deploying editing environments at lower cost, but they lack the flexibility and agility that comes with architecting a custom solution from individual components. As appropriate, you can leverage dedicated and custom environments side-by-side, to use the best technologies for the different users in your organization.

A live and post production environment that provides remote access by leveraging cloud and virtualization technologies is comprised of several components, illustrated in Figure 1.

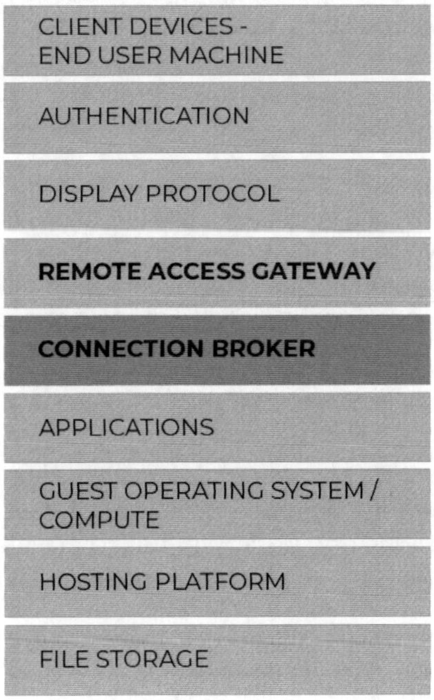


FIGURE 1: OVERVIEW OF A REMOTE ACCESS STACK FOR LIVE AND POST PRODUCTION WORKLOADS.

Note that this discussion does not cover applications and file storage, other than to point out that typically the applications and data are hosted near each other to improve the application performance.

[1] AWS, Amazon EC2, and EC2 are trademarks of Amazon.com, Inc. or its affiliates in the United States and/or other countries.

The goal in this article is to discuss architecting a remote access solution to connect users to the applications and data. Doing so requires the components described in the following sections.

### Hosting Platforms

The foundation of a remote access architecture is the platform running the operating systems and applications. This can be comprised of physical workstations hosted in a data center, virtual machines running on-premises in a virtualization layer, or cloud workstations running in any of the available clouds. A hybrid environment leverages different platforms side by side as best suited to the user's task.

### Guest Operating System and Compute

Not all applications run on every type of operating systems, and different applications require different levels of GPU, CPU, and RAM. Hybrid environments often include a mixture of Microsoft® Windows®, Apple® macOS®, and Linux® operating system software, hosted on physical hardware, virtual workstations, or cloud workstations.[2] Your remote access platform must be architected to support connections to all types of guest operating systems.

### Connection Broker

Connection brokers are the gatekeepers of hosted live and post production environments, integrating with authentication servers to authorize access for the appropriate users and defining access control rules that permit connections to the correct set of hosted workstations. In cloud environments, the connection broker is also responsible for automating tasks related to bursting capacity and managing power state to minimize compute costs. The connection broker must integrate with all of the other components in the remote access solution to simplify administration and provide a seamless end-user experience.

### Remote Access Gateway

Historically, organizations provided remote access to corporate workstations using a VPN. However, the increase in remote workers proved that VPNs are unable to provide an easily managed solution with the performance required for live and post production workflows in a cost-effective manner. Gateways dedicated to remote access platforms provide secure connections to cloud or on-premises workstations, based on the access control rules defined in the connection broker managing the gateway.

### Display Protocol

The display protocol is the key to content security and end-user satisfaction. In simple terms, it transports pixels from the hosted workstation to the user's client device. Different display protocols provide different levels of customizations and performance, so are better suited for different environments.

### Authentication

Authentication servers are responsible for verifying the user's identity in order for the connection broker to implement access control rules based on the user's authentication server attributes. Authentication can be single or multi-factor, using any number of identity providers based on your corporate standards.

---

[2] Linux is the registered trademark of Linus Torvalds in the U.S. and other countries. Microsoft and Windows are registered trademarks of Microsoft Corporation in the United States and/or other countries. Apple, macOS, and Mac are registered trademarks of Apple Inc., registered in the U.S. and other countries and regions.

### Client Devices

The client is any device used to log into the remote access environment, for example Zero clients, laptops, and Web browsers. When considering remote users, often the client device is outside of the control of the IT administrator. In other cases, organizations provide Zero clients to end users, for additional security.

These components link together in an architecture that can span cloud regions, as conceptually shown in Figure 2. The remainder of this article discusses important considerations when choosing the appropriate technology to use for these various components in your architecture.

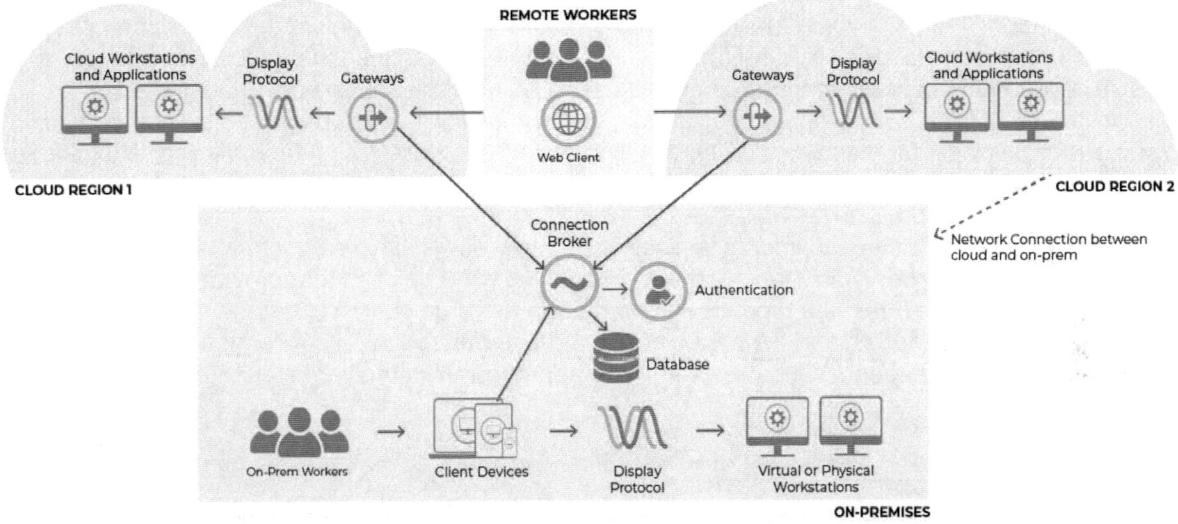


FIGURE 2: CONCEPTUAL ARCHITECTURE OF A HYBRID REMOTE ACCESS PLATFORM FOR LIVE AND POST-PRODUCTION.

## Selecting a Hosting Platform

Where you choose to host your workstations forms the foundation of your remote access platform. Historically, these workstations lived under a desk, belonging to a particular editor or shared by a project team. Over time, the workstations moved into the data center, potentially with an expensive KVM device providing connections from the user's desk or from shared editing bays or rooms. As vGPU technologies evolved, organizations began to virtualize workstations, either using on-premises virtualization or a public cloud.

All four of these options: 1) dedicated workstations; 2) hosted, shared workstations; 3) on-premises virtualization; and 4) cloud-hosted workstations remain in use and useful, depending on your location, situation, and use cases.

### Dedicated Workstations

Many organizations have existing investments in dedicated workstations, and including these systems in your remote access solution until they reach their end-of-life allows you to maximize your return on investment. Moving forward, you may continue to have some use cases, particularly for applications running on macOS operating system software, where it is still beneficial to dedicate a workstation to a particular user or to a particular station in a lab or room.

Workstations that are dedicated to a particular user are easily managed by any remote access platform that can model one-to-one assignments of workstations to users. For workstations at a shared desk (such as in a lab), balancing the workstation's use between on-premises users and users logging in remotely is a key benefit of including a connection broker in your remote access solution.

Some organizations, Leostream learned, physically move dedicated workstations to different rooms or stations as VFX or other teams change projects. These workstations are ideal candidates to replace with virtualized or cloud-hosted workstations, discussed later.

### Hosted Workstations

Hosted workstations reside in your datacenter and are often shared among users as part of a pool of resources. Pooled workstations are ideal for applications that are not used in day-to-day work, or for expensive applications that are shared by multiple users, as examples. Pooled workstations can be over-allocated by using a connection broker to manage access for the group of users. Using pooled workstations maximizes the machine's utility, allowing you to purchase less hardware and require less infrastructure to support them.

Hosted workstations are also used in on-premises screening rooms, where editors can work with their customers. Often, these rooms are equipped with expensive KVM devices that provide access to specific workstations, rendering the room useful for certain tasks. In some cases, the KVM device can be replaced with a client device and the mini-cinema can be wrapped into your remote access solution, with the connection broker connecting the user to the appropriate hosted workstation based on their task.

### Virtualized Workstations

Virtualized workstations provide a way to save money by hosting multiple workstations on a single server, sharing the GPU of the underlying hardware. They are less expensive then dedicated workstations and are a particularly good alternative to using a cloud-hosted workstation in regions where the cloud is not as advanced and, therefore, more expensive and perhaps without peering or direct-connect options.

### Cloud Workstations

As remote access becomes increasingly important, the cloud is gaining more and more traction. Cloud workstations deliver a number of benefits above and beyond the other workstation types listed above. Particularly in the face of supply chain delays and chip shortages, cloud workstations are a faster and more predictable way to provide editors with a workstation. Also, using the cloud allows IT to respond faster to requests from users and clients. Finally, the inherit elasticity of the cloud makes it ideal for bursting when additional compute is temporarily required, avoiding the investment and time required to purchase new hardware and equip a data center to hold it.

Ideally, your remote access solution and the connection broker included in it should be capable of managing any of the workstation options listed here.

When choosing what workloads to host on different platforms in a hybrid solution, consider the following:

- How do you keep the data close to the applications that use it? If the data is on-premises, it may be best to keep the users' tasks and workstations on-premises.
- Where are users located? If the cloud is not as advanced in their region, on-premises virtualized workstations may be a better cost-saving option.

- Do you have a relationship with a cloud vendor to lower the cost for storage and I/O at scale? If so, rendering in the cloud becomes a more attractive option.
- Are you building a disaster recovery (DR) solution? The cloud represents a perfect location for DR as instances that are powered down incur very low costs.

Unless you leverage a dedicated cloud solution for live and post production workflows, you must define the requirements of your cloud-hosted workstations, including:

- GPU
- vCPUs
- Memory
- Region

Based on those requirements, select the appropriate instance size provided by your cloud vendor.

## Managing Cloud Costs

By and large, compute represents the largest cost associated with running Media & Entertainment workloads in the cloud. As mentioned previously, you can work with your cloud provider to help minimize costs associated with storage and data I/O. To help minimize compute costs, integrate a connection broker into your remote access environment that automates tasks related to capacity and power state.

### Optimizing Capacity

When utilizing a cloud environment, as much as possible, keep capacity at a minimum until it is required by the creatives and editors. This rule-of-thumb applies not just when bursting additional capacity, but also for planning normal day-to-day load. Some considerations as you design your environment:

- Do you have projects, shows, or employees working on known schedules? If so, you can plan to have compute available at the time these shifts start. This way, the editors do not have to wait for their resource to start, but that resource is not incurring costs until you can bill for that project.
- Do you have quotas on the amount of compute a client may consume? If so, ensure you place a cap on the number of instances that can be launched for that client.
- Can you treat your compute as ephemeral? If no data is stored on the instance, consider terminating the instances as soon as the user completes their task and logs out.

### Automating Power State

Because compute costs are incurred when an instance is running, it's not always necessary to terminate the instance to save money. In many cases, automatically powering down the instance when the user's task is complete is sufficient.

Here, the key is to remember that users, themselves, will never consistently remember to logout or power down their machines. Instead, leverage a connection broker to monitor the state of the user's connection to the workstation, and power it down when appropriate, for example:

- When the user logs out of the operating system, schedule an automatic power down after a delay, to give the user leeway to log back in quickly if they have unfinished work.
- If the user disconnects their remote session, monitor for a reconnect and, if none occurs, power down the instance.

- Monitor how long the user's session is idle, to catch cases when the user leaves their system unattended, and automatically power down the machine if no significant tasks are running in the background.

By carefully automating capacity and power state, you can minimize compute costs in the cloud. In addition, keeping machines that are not in use powered down removes attack vectors in your environment, increasing the security of your overall system.

## Choosing Display Protocols

A remote display protocol transfers the display of the remote workstation to the user's client device. It is the key to the end-user experience, as well as to the security of your remote access solution. In the words of a Leostream customer, your environment is "only as secure as is your protocol".

At a high-level, all display protocols fall into two categories: 1) commodity protocols such as Microsoft RDP or VNC or 2) high-performance display protocols such as NICE DCV or Teradici® PCoIP®. Commodity display protocols are often low or no cost and are adequate for many tasks. They typically are not adequate for tasks that require audio/video syncing.

In this case, and generally for more accurate 3-D rendering, choose a high-performance display protocol. While audio/video sync remains a challenge, Leostream customers indicated that display protocols such as Teradici PCoIP and HP® ZCentral Remote Boost are good options for these workloads. Factors such as the frequency of the monitor can play a role in how well the audio and video remain in sync, so consider tuning these parameters to improve the display protocol performance.

High performance display protocols typically require additional licensing, but there are ways to minimize this cost. For example, Remote Boost licenses are included with HP Z Workstations, making it a cost-effective option for organizations that standardize on HP hardware. NICE DCV is gaining traction for use with Amazon EC2, as the DCV license is included in the EC2 compute costs.

A common theme among Leostream Media & Entertainment customers, however, is that content security is more important than licensing cost, latency, and efficiency. Display protocols transfer pixels, not data, and the traffic from the remote host to the client device is secured via encryption. The security hole to plug, then, is between the end user and the remote workstation.

In order to keep data on the remote workstation, look for a display protocol that provides control over drive redirection, cut-and-paste, clipart, and other features that provide a way for users to transfer data from the remote workstation to their local device. Also consider the directionality of these features. For example, you may want artists to be able to copy a texture from their local client to the remote workstation, but do not want them to be able to copy textures in the other direction.

When investigating display protocols for your remote access environment, consider the following:

- What remote operating systems are users connecting to? NoMachine is a popular option for users connecting to remote macOS operating system software, with Penguin Computing® Scyld Cloud Workstation™ and Teradici PCoIP providing other options for remote Apple Mac® computers.
- Do you need to support session collaboration? Not all display protocols currently support multiple users collaborating on the same remote session. Mechdyne TGX™, NICE DCV, NoMachine, and HP ZCentral Remote Boost currently support this functionality. For other display protocols, you can leverage a third-party system for collaboration, but these systems may not integrate into your complete remote access solution.

- How tunable do you need the display protocol to be? The more options for tuning the display protocol, the better you can adjust its performance and feature set to satisfy your needs.
- What type of client devices will end users have and can they install software on these devices? Some display protocols, such as NICE DCV, NoMachine, and Scyld Cloud Workstation provide HTML5 viewers, removing the need to install and update software clients.

Display protocols continue to evolve, for example the demand for remote editing over the pandemic led to advances that resolved issues delivering pen pressure to the remote workstation. The key for a robust remote access solution is to be able to mix and match display protocols based on the particular needs of a user and project, and to have the agility and flexibility to change how the display protocol is configured or switch to a new option as requirements and feature sets change.

## Enabling Collaboration

When referring to remote access, collaboration can take on many meanings. This discussion covers two use cases. First, video conferencing collaboration is a mainstay in today's remote work environments. For users working on-premises in production environments with no network access, this type of collaboration is impossible. In a remote work environment, users have the best of both worlds. They can securely connect to their production environment using your remote access solution, then use their network-connected client device to access their video conferencing system. Users who could not previously communicate in real-time, can do so easily while working remotely.

Second, some projects benefit when users can work in real-time on the project by collaborating within the workstation, itself. In this case, two remote users connect to and view the same display, and are able to interact with the application running on the workstation to make edits. For users sitting side-by-side, this type of collaboration is natural. For remote workers, this type of collaboration requires a display protocol that supports multiple users connecting to the same session. Some display protocols that support this functionality include:

- HP ZCentral Remote Boost
- Mechdyne TGX
- NICE DCV
- NoMachine
- Scyld Cloud Workstation

When allowing remote collaboration, it is imperative that you have insight into which users are working together, what workstations and projects are actively being collaborated on, and when these collaborations are taking place. This type of insight is easy to glean when collaborations are tracked by the connection broker used in your remote access environment. The connection broker not only provides insight for IT, it can simplify the end-user experience by providing ways for users to request others to collaborate on their session.

If your environment requires users to collaborate on remote sessions, consider the following:

- Are you committed to a display protocol and, if so, does it support remote collaboration? If not, consider integrating a second display protocol with collaboration support into your environment.
- Can you limit users to collaborating only with other users in their project? You can increase the security of your environment by only allowing collaboration through your remote access connection broker and using the broker as a guide for who is allowed to collaborate together.
- What level of reporting do you require to track collaborations?

## Connecting Remote Users

The increase in remote work quickly exposed the downside of using VPNs for external access to internal systems. Client devices that connect via a VPN have open access to the production network, and therefore must be treated as managed devices and be compliant with corporate security policies, such as running required anti-virus software. In addition, the VPN is a performance bottleneck as the number of users connecting through the device increases.

Building a performant and scalable remote access solution requires a gateway purpose-built for connections to hosted workstations. The gateway connects users to their workstation using the chosen display protocol. Instructions on who can connect, what they can connect to, where they can connect from, and how long the connection persists, are sent to the gateway by the connection broker, creating a secure yet automated system for remote access.

When you include a gateway in the platform managing access to your workstations, you open up a wide range of new use cases. For example, a remote access solution that connects users through a gateway managed by a connection broker makes it easier for IT to on-board new employees or contractors. Organizations can essentially hire specialized talent and source contractors on-demand, from anywhere, and expedite their on-boarding to handle project-based workloads. Outsourced artists can be provided a login account for the remote access platform and connected to their offered workstation, instead of being fully integrated into the production environment.

As another example, gateways can be used to provide access for remote developers working on an internal Gitlab repository. The developer connects to and works on their remote workstation, so the code base is never pulled onto their personal device.

Lastly, using cloud hosted workstations accessed through gateways allows organizations to scale to satisfy a global workforce. Workstations can be isolated in private networks in regions around the world, with connections available through the appropriate gateway for each region. IT can easily reassign creatives and editors to new projects or sites by changing the user's access control rules in the connection broker, which then routes the user to the correct gateway and remote workstation.

When looking for and architecting a gateway into your remote access platform, consider the following:

- What display protocol or protocols are you considering? Some gateways are purpose-built for particular display protocols while others can handle a variety of display protocols. You can mix and match these gateways in your environment, but should be aware of any architectural constraints that arise from doing so.
- How many users will need to connect through your gateways? The number of users that can simultaneously connect through a single gateway depends on the type of connections being sent through that gateway. For graphically intense workloads, the bandwidth of the gateway's network is a critical factor when determining the number of simultaneous users that a gateway can support. Larger environments require multiple gateways, managed by a load balancer.
- Where are the users' workstations located? Each gateway provides connections to a particular network of workstations. Large-scale global environments need to leverage multiple gateways to distribute load and provide connections to different clouds or regions.

## Building Zero-Trust Architectures

A common theme among all Leostream customers is to architect with security in mind, from authenticating the user, to defining access control rules that indicate what workstations they may access, to monitoring constantly. The need for content security translates into a requirement to architect your remote access solution with zero-trust constructs in mind.

To design for zero trust, you must assume all users and devices are untrusted, require strict authentication, and define comprehensive access control rules to indicate who may access hosted workstations from where. Security gateways, discussed in the previous section, are a key component of zero-trust architectures as they allow you to treat the user's client as an untrusted device, by removing the VPN that otherwise allows the client device onto your internal network.

Next, you need to establish trust in your users, which is done using your corporate authentication servers and identify providers. Robust authentication, including multi-factor authentication for remote users, is critical for securing remote access. The remote access platform that enables connections to your remote workstation must be able to leverage your corporate systems to authentication users, and allow you to leverage different authentication methods as potentially required by different teams, projects, or locations.

The user's location is a key factor in defining the level of trust a user is permitted. You may consider forcing remote users to pass stricter authentication levels than users who are on-premises. You may also want to change what the user is allowed to access, based on where they log in from.

This is the final zero-trust construct that is important in a remote access platform; access control rules that determine what remote resources the user may connect to based on the user's trusted identity and their current location. Controlling remote access based on where the user logs in from allows you to deny or change access as the user moves from site to site, and prevent administrative tasks when the user is remote.

A remote workstation solution architected with zero trust in mind then needs to monitor constantly, as described in the next section, so you are aware of who is using what resource from where, so you can be proactive to breaches or problems.

To summarize, to design your remote access solution with zero-trust concepts in mind, consider the following:

- How will you establish trust in your users? Often username/password authentication is not sufficient and you need to integrate one or more MFA providers into your remote access solution.
- How does the user's location change what they may access? Location-awareness is critical not just for changing what remote workstations the user may access, but also for monitoring usage patterns to discover potential problems, such as attempted access from unexpected locations.
- Do you need to restrict access based on time-of-day? For projects or shows that run over a known time span, you can decrease attack vectors by allowing access to those remote workstations only during the time the project or show is running.

## Tracking Resource Usage

Tracking remote access to hosted resources is an important consideration when architecting your overall solution. Tracking figures into discussions about content security, accountability, and potentially billing if you are delivering editing solutions for clients.

Because security is key for pre-release content, the connection broker included in your remote access solution needs to monitor and log who is logging in, for how long, and if they left a machine sitting idle. These insights allow you to be in tune with how all sites are operating, and discover any outlying behaviors that could indicate a breach.

When working with clients, detailed logs are critical during security audits, as well as for accurately billing based on usage. Accurate logs indicate exactly when a user started consuming a workstation, so you can bill the client as soon as work begins.

When tracking remote access, consider the following:

- Can you monitor for idle users, as well as for logins, logouts, and disconnects? Ideally, you want to track all of these events and potentially automate actions so you can forcefully log out idle users, for example.
- Can you track where users are logging in from? If you log the location of the user's client device, you can look for trends in where users are working from and block remote access from undesired locations.
- What user access trends are important for your organization? Accurate resource usage reports allow you to analyze your environment to see what systems may be over or under allocated, allowing you to shift workstations to different tasks if they are consistently unused for their current project, for example.

## Conclusion

There are many considerations when architecting a remote access solution for a hybrid live and post production environment, as presented in this article. There is no one-size-fits-all solution, however, there is a common theme that having one management platform for IT and end users to access everything simplifies the day-to-day operation of the system. Delivery, maintenance, the type of desktop, the display protocol, etc., will be different for each organization and even for sites within an organization. Architecting a solution with scalability and elasticity in mind is the key to building next-generation creative studios.

# Can I Really Protect My Broadcast Plant from a Cybersecurity Attack?

**Wayne M. Pecena**
**Texas A&M University - KAMU TV/FM**
**College Station, Texas, United States**
w-pecena@tamu.edu

**Abstract** – IP networks are a fundamental building block of the broadcast technical plant. Integration with the legacy broadcast infrastructure can range from minimal system control functions to an end-to-end IP based content transport facility. Regardless of the level of integration, cybersecurity cannot be ignored to insure a reliable, secure and protected system.

Industry cybersecurity principals are commonly based upon a complex framework of principles from the National Institute of Standards and Technology (NIST). The NIST Framework is often a complex and a daunting task to implement within a broadcast facility. An effective cybersecurity programs begins with the design of the network.

This paper and presentation will provide an understanding of practical implementable cybersecurity precautions based upon the NIST Framework for the broadcast station. Specific topics to be addressed will include an overall understanding of cybersecurity principles and a step-by-step infrastructure implementation guide for the broadcast facility whether large or small. The guide will be focused upon a secure network design approach, the use of Ethernet switch security capabilities, the use of packet filtering and firewalls and an understanding of implementing common cybersecurity threat mitigation techniques.

## Introduction to Cybersecurity

The migration of the broadcast plant to an IT based infrastructure has brought many advantages to the broadcast station. System flexibility, enhanced feature availability and cost are often found in the list of advantages. As a result, the broadcast plant has become an Information Technology (IT) infrastructure based upon the Internet Protocol (IP) for interconnection, servers that capture, process and playout content and a cadre of specialized host devices that provide the specialized services required in the broadcast workflow. These host devices are computers at heart executing customized software that perform the functions required. The era of the customized hardware design has been replaced with the use of generic off-the-shelf IT hardware and software defining the current and future device and system capabilities.

Now that we are entrenched in an IT infrastructure, there are new challenges that must be embraced. Cybersecurity is one front and foremost challenge faced by the broadcast IT engineer. The broadcast industry has been relatively untouched for decades even as the technology employed migrated from analog to digital. The infrastructure traditionally employed baseband signals of analog audio and video, digital audio and video that were built on dedicated infrastructure. The dedicated infrastructure might be shielded twisted-pair cabling, coaxial cable or even fiber optics. A key attribute that it was dedicated in

This paper is excerpted from the Proceedings of the 2021 NAB Broadcast Engineering and Information Technology (BEIT) Conference, © 2021, National Association of Broadcasters, 1 M Street S.E., Washington, DC 20003 USA.

a point-point arrangement for interconnection rather than a shared infrastructure utilized among multiple devices and functions. With everything now IP based, we have a common infrastructure that transports packets regardless of the payload they might contain. The advantage of the IT infrastructure arises. Cybersecurity is simply an area that must be addressed rather than ignored. The threats to the IT infrastructure that exist today are numerous and widespread. From a high-level view, threats can be categorized into malware or network focused threats. Malware threats focus upon the host operating system and applications they execute. Common industry sub-categories of malware include:

- Ransomware
- Viruses
- Worms and Trojans
- Spyware

Network focused threats focus upon the network infrastructure components and exploiting the IP protocol(s) that include threats such as:

- Address Resolution Protocol (ARP) spoofing
- Rogue service advertisements
- Denial of Service (DoS) attacks
- Distributed Denial of Service (DDoS) attacks
- Man in the Middle attacks

Today, the DDoS attack and ransomware likely offer the greatest threat to any IT system, broadcast focused or not. Sources of these threats can originate from many sources or actors. Threat sources include:

- Nation states
- Terrorist groups & organizations
- Organized crime
- Hacktivists
- Hackers
- Disgruntled individuals

The sheer number of potential threats combined with the diversity of threat sources often ends in a feeling of a hopeless situation and results in throwing one's hands up admitting defeat. Cybersecurity is and can be extremely complex and countless financial resources can be consumed in attempts to prevent and mitigate the impact upon our broadcast plant. Hope should not be lost, as there are effective and often inexpensive steps that can be taken to prevent a cybersecurity event from occurring or to minimize the impact if an event occurs.

Cybersecurity is often defined as "focused upon the protection of computers, networks, programs and data from change, destruction or unauthorized access and/or change." A first step in the elimination of the cybersecurity helpless mindset can be found in an understanding of a few cybersecurity principles followed by a structured approach to implementing prevention measures.

## Principles of Cybersecurity

The National Institute of Standards and Technology (NIST) Cybersecurity Framework provides structured guidelines and steps to implement and maintain ongoing cybersecurity programs in any organization. [1] The framework is comprised of five (5) functional categories describing the following high-level functional areas of a cybersecurity program:

- Identify
- Protect

- Detect
- Respond
- Recovery

Each of the five functional categories are further sub-divided into levels of further detail leading to implementable steps through an extensive set of reference documents. These references provide the implementation detail appropriate for the specific level. Figure 1 illustrates the five functional categories and the first-level of sub-categories of the framework.

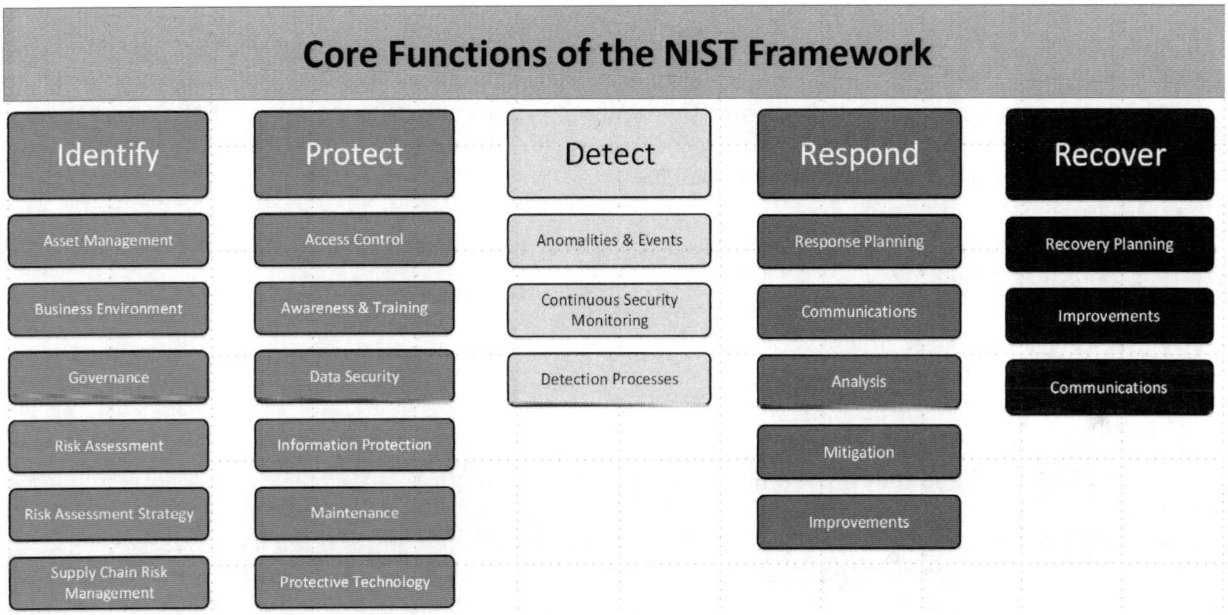


FIGURE 1: THE NIST CYBERSECURITY FRAMEWORK.

The Identity function begins with an accurate account of all IT assets involved. IT assets include hardware, software, networks, and data. From the inventory produced, the assets are in turn prioritized based upon the organizations business context. Reliable delivery of program content is likely a high-priority business context for any broadcast station. The identity process is the first step of implementing a risk-based plan and the first step in dispelling the helpless mindset by bringing structure and dividing a complex undertaking into manageable steps. A risk based analysis approach does not seek to address every IT cybersecurity risk that may exist at the same priority level. It seeks to identify and assign a high priority to the high impact and high likelihood potential threats. Less priority is assigned to the lower impact and lesser likelihood threats. A numerical rating scale is often used to describe the overall cybersecurity health of an organization's IT systems. Areas found deficient can then be used to prioritize resources to remedy or bring into compliance in situations where regulatory requirements or organizational policy exists.

The Protect function utilizes the previously compiled IT asset inventory to create a policy or approach of what to protect and how to protect an asset. Asset protection is addressed in terms of physical asset protection as well as establishing access control for users and applications. The concept of least privilege required is utilized.

The Detect function is focused upon IT asset monitoring in terms of knowing what is normal and alerting when an anomaly occurs. In this functional area, the systems are identified that are required to monitor system activity or user activity alerting when a possible cybersecurity event occurs.

The Respond function focuses upon a plan of action when a breech occurs. The scope ranges from a physical event such as a facility break-in to a malware incident occurring. Recovery steps are identified in advance such that recovery can be as efficient as possible as opposed to developing a plan after an event occurs. The post-analysis aspect of any event occurrence is also an important step in the continued improvement process.

The last functional area addressed is Recovery in scope with the Response action plan, the Recovery function outlines steps to restore compromised assets and return to normal operation.

The National Security Agency (NSA) developed the principle of Defense in Depth (DiD). [2] DiD provides the concept of multi-layered coordinated security mechanisms to implement. The goal is to have redundancy in protection mechanisms. The concept is based upon the premise that if one security protection mechanism fails or is breeched another obstacle is in place. Practical examples of DiD mechanisms found in IT infrastructures can include:

- Physical access barriers
- Segmented (layered) network architecture
- Ethernet port security
- Packet filtering through an Access Control List (ACL)
- Packet filtering via a firewall
- Encryption
- Virtual Private Networks (VPN)
- Authentication & access control
- Protection systems (antivirus, malware, intrusion detection)

The architecture of a castle can best illustrate the DiD concept. Often surrounded by a moat, an attacker might be faced with armed guard towers and an outer barrier wall if the moat as the first barrier is breeched. If the outer wall is breeched, the attacker is likely to find a higher inner wall to conquer. All of these barriers are in place to protect the treasures stored in the most inner core of the castle.

The Principle of Least Privilege (PoLP) establishes that a security architecture should be designed to grant the minimal resources required for a user or an application to perform the desired system function. PoLP is implemented through access controls for allowing authorized users to access specific systems or an application to have file modification permissions as examples.

The CIA triad is often considered the classic model of IT security. The model utilizes three (3) objectives to be achieved within any IT system ranging from the network to the server storage systems to the applications. The three objectives are illustrated in Figure 2 and are comprised of:

- Confidentiality
- Integrity
- Availability

Confidentiality can be equated to privacy or preventing information to reaching undesired hands or unauthorized users. Access by users and applications is restricted or limited to a “need-to-access.” Other IT system implementation techniques include encryption, authentication and off-line data storage.

Integrity seeks to prevent data from being changed as it moves through a network, is processed through an IT workflow or as stored at rest in a data storage system. File access controls, checksums and encryption are common implementation mechanisms. An important aspect of the Integrity objective is to have detection mechanism(s) to know if tampering or altercation has occurred.

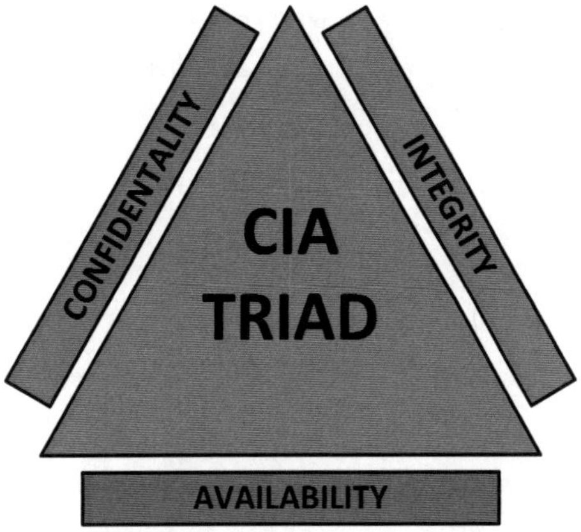


FIGURE 2: THE CIA TRIAD.

Availability seeks to ensure that IT resources are available to legitimate users or applications and not available to those that are not authorized to access or utilize. Implementation techniques include network infrastructure redundancy, server redundancy and attack detection systems.

It is important to note that that the acronym CIA is not referring to the United States Government Central Intelligence Agency. You may find the concept labeled as the "AIC" Triad to avoid any confusion. The triad seems to have evolved through various Information Security (infosec) professionals over a 10–12 year period beginning with a 1976 Air Force paper popularizing the Identity concept to the Availability objective in 1988 after the introduction of the Morris computer worm. [3].

Whereas the triad becomes an objective roadmap for the broadcast IT engineer seeking to protect their broadcast infrastructure from cybersecurity attacks, the CIA triad is used as a target roadmap for those seeking to do harm to IT systems and the broadcast plant operation. Now Confidentiality becomes a target to be breeched to obtain valuable information or expose sensitive data through techniques such as social-engineering or spyware. Integrity becomes a target of Man-in-the-Middle attacks, malware and data record manipulation. Availability becomes the primary objective of a ransomware infection or a Denial of Service (DoS/DDoS) attack.

## Protecting the Broadcast Infrastructure

An awareness of the cybersecurity threats that exist and a basic understanding of key cybersecurity principles provide the foundation to implement cybersecurity protections in a structured and coordinated manner. A high-level view of an organization's IT infrastructure can be divided into three areas, each with unique cybersecurity needs. Whereas this paper will focus upon the network, host device and applications cybersecurity protections will be briefly addressed.

The Open Systems Interconnection (OSI) model developed in the early 80's is the classic model that describes how host devices communicate with each other over a network. [4] Considered a legacy model by some, the OSI model provides an excellent structure in which to implement cybersecurity precautions. The first 4 layers as illustrated in Figure 3 of the model are referred to as the data-flow layers and are associated with the network functions.

The network architecture is the starting point for cybersecurity precaution implementation. Layer 1 or the physical layer of the OSI model is generally associated with the physical type of network deployed. Options today are all Ethernet based and includes wired through twisted-pair copper cabling, fiber optic cabling, wireless or a combination of all three in many networks. From a security standpoint, the physical layer can also be applied to physical security of the network infrastructure equipment. Typical implementation can include locked wiring closet equipment cabinets, locked rack cabinets shared space or a dedicated “IT” room with controlled access.

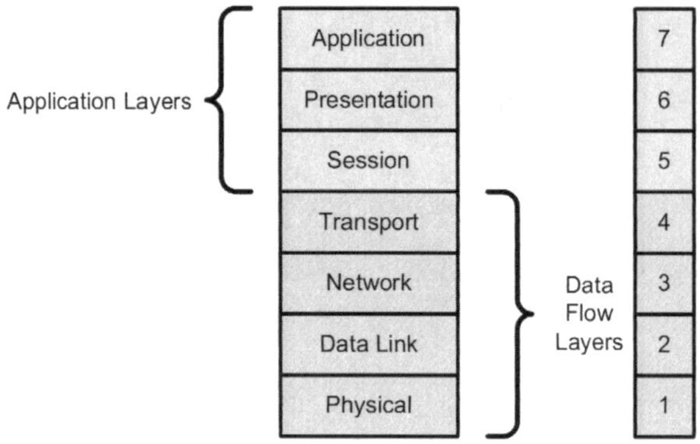


FIGURE 3: THE OSI MODEL.

The physical layer can also be applied to the network architecture or design of the network. Traditional network design was based upon a “flat” network approach where all host devices have the same access and are addressed to the same network or subnet. The current network design approach recommends a layered or segmented approach to the network architecture. Advantages of a segmented network design include performance enhancements and increased security. Performance enhancement is beyond the scope of this paper, but in general focused upon minimizing unnecessary broadcast network traffic. The cybersecurity advantages focus on the ability to minimize the attack surface and controlling access to hosts. In practice, the segmented network architecture approach groups hosts in functional layers based upon security priority. An example of a segmented network that could be found in the broadcast plant is illustrated in Figure 4.

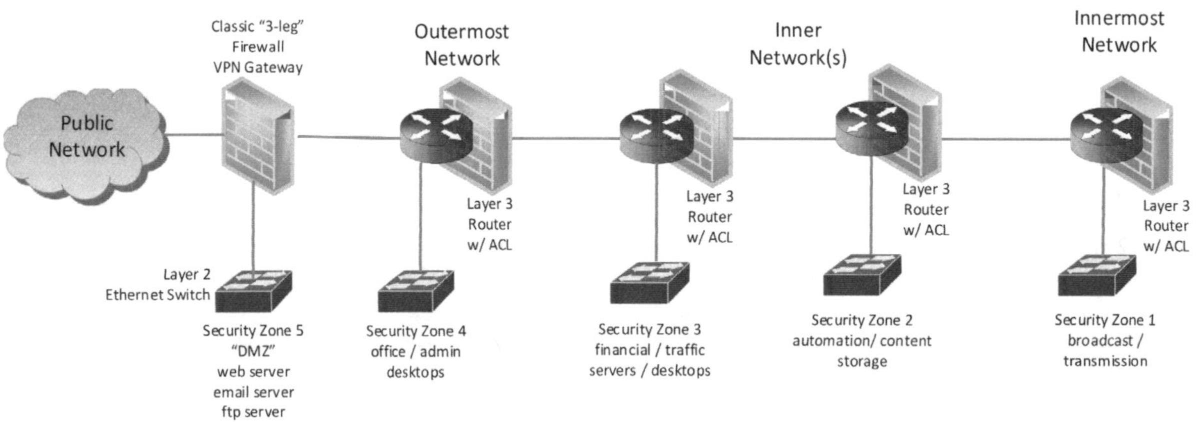


FIGURE 4: THE SEGMENTED OR LAYER NETWORK.

The segmented network adheres to the cybersecurity principle of Defense in Depth and a fundamental recommendation in adopting the NIST Cybersecurity framework. If a breech should occur in the outermost network, another barrier is presented as well as limiting the reach of attack to those hosts only on the compromised network. In the case of a ransomware event, the spread of the malware is limited or contained to that individual network rather than the entire network within the organization. In practice the Virtual Local Area Network (VLAN) becomes the primary tool for implementing a segmented network architecture. The VLAN approach allows a single physical network to support multiple sub-networks or subnets. Each subnet is an isolated individual network with its own addressing assignments. At this point, there is no communications or interoperability between subnets. If required, subnet interoperability will be added in a controlled manner by use of Layer 3 routing and Access Control List (ACL) techniques addressed later in this paper.

Upon first glance, the network illustrated would require numerous network devices to implement. In reality, the network illustrated could be built with two network devices. A firewall appliance handles the border protection, DMZ provisioning and VPN access. The remaining Ethernet switching and IP routing can be provided by a single "Layer 3 switch" with adequate port capacity. With 48-port switches commonplace, small network needs can be met in a single device. If additional capacity is needed, expansion can be accommodated by additional standalone Ethernet switches or use of a chassis-based switch platform with the appropriate quantity of switch port interface card(s) installed. It is important to note that a Layer 3 switch is a marketing term associated with a single network device that performs traditional Ethernet switching and IP routing on a port-by-port basis.

After Layer 1 or the physical layer, Layer 2 or the data-link layer provides an opportunity for another layer of protection. With a VLAN based segmented network implemented, the use of a managed Ethernet switch is implied. The managed Ethernet switch allows the custom configuration of VLAN(s) as well as providing several cybersecurity features. A fundamental cybersecurity feature is Ethernet switch port security. Port security provides the ability to limit or restrict what host device can be attached to a switch port. A fundamental role of the Ethernet switch is to learn a host device Media Access Control (MAC) address. The MAC address is the physical address of an Ethernet based host device and is "burned-in" the device firmware. The learned MAC address is captured from an incoming frame and stored along with the switch port number in the switch internal MAC address table or Content Addressable Memory (CAM) table.

If a foreign device should be attached to a switch port, the switch automatically responds upon detection of a foreign MAC address. A typical switch response would be to shut-down or disable the port involved, drop the received Ethernet frame and send a notification to the broadcast IT engineer that a violation has occurred. In essence, Ethernet port security provides another barrier if physical tampering occurs, and a foreign device is connected to the network switch port. A best practice approach allows a single host to be connected to a switch port by limiting to a single MAC address per switch port. This limiting step can also help to minimize the impact of a DoS attack by preventing the Ethernet switch CAM table overflow. A switch will re-boot if a CAM table overflow should occur.

The managed Ethernet switch can provide additional security features such as Dynamic Host Control Protocol (DHCP) snooping which can detect and prevent a rogue DHCP server to be attached to the network. This could occur during a Man in the Middle cybersecurity event or simply as an accident when improperly connecting a Wireless Access Point (WAP) to a switch. A practical example is the connection of the WAP WAN port to a network cable rather than the LAN port, thus adding the WAP DHCP or rogue functionality to the network. DHCP snooping essentially acts as a DHCP firewall.

After Layer 2 or the data-link layer, Layer 3 or the network layer brings another level of protection opportunity and functionality to the overall network infrastructure. The network layer is associated with virtual addressing (IP address), inter-network routing and packet filtering. Additional cybersecurity protection can be implemented through IP Security (IPsec) encryption. As noted in the Layer 1 paragraph, interoperability between the segmented networks must be added when necessary. Layer 3 routing must be enabled or implemented to provide the desired inter-subnet communications. Routing is only added when required and if implanted it is controlled via packet filtering through an Access Control List (ACL).

The ACL is critical to controlling access to a subnet or network by performing basic packet filtering. The ACL will either permit or deny an IP packet from entering a Layer 3 device ingress interface or leaving an egress interface. The admit or deny decision is based upon a pre-defined rule that utilizes the IP layer 3 header information such as source IP address, destination IP address or protocol. The IP address can be a single address, a logical block of IP addresses such as a subnet as defined by the IP address subnet mask. With the additional information provided by Layer 4 or the transport layer the decision, the permit or deny decision can include port information. The transport port number often associated with a specific service or application communications. Logical operator statements can be used in an ACL to allow logical combination of Layer 3 and 4 header information to reach the permit or deny decision. Creating the ACL can be complex and often time consuming, it is very effective once in place and acts as a stateless firewall.

In addition to an ACL, a conventional Layer 3 firewall can be implemented between internal subnets. A distinct difference between an ACL and a conventional firewall is the stateful operation of the firewall. The firewall will in general deny incoming packets from an outside network unless an internal network host originated the conversation with the outside host. The firewall remembers the conversation through an internal table dynamically created for each conversation created. In practice the firewall will incorporate both stateless permit or deny rules such as found in an ACL and dynamic rules that are created based upon stateful conversations where allowed. A practical example could be an automation system in a subnet requesting the daily programming log from a traffic system located in another subnet. The ACL would allow only the two hosts to communicate via the File Transfer Protocol (FTP).

IP by original design is not secure. To secure, encryption or IP Security (IPsec) must be added. IPsec is a Layer 3 encryption technique that provided secure communications between host devices. Encryption can be implemented at several levels of the OSI model, with Layer 3 or IPsec forming the foundation encryption. It should be noted that Layer 2 encryption is possible and often utilized by the government and military applications. Layer 2 encryption is accomplished by dedicated proprietary hardware "green" boxes and not typically found in the commercial market industries primarily due to cost.

Encryption should be used any time a public network such as the Internet is utilized for communications with another network such as remote access via a Virtual Private Network (VPN). Encryption can also be used in internal networks such as an IP based Studio-Transmitter-Link (STL) path. This is yet another method to prevent unauthorized access or disruption of information transported and/or a Man in the Middle attack to disrupt normal programming. Encryption is also available at Layer 4 as Transport Layer Security (TLS) and at Layer 7 as application security such as Secure Sockets Layer (SSL). SSL is based upon creating an authenticated and encrypted communications link between hosts such as a user client exchange with an application server.

Protecting the host device is often complex due to the diversity and sheer number of potential devices encountered. An IP host device can take on numerous forms and functions. Traditionally, a host has been a server or desktop computer. Today, the variety of possible devices is vast. Regardless, they all share common characteristics and capabilities as defined by the Internet Engineering Task Force (IETF) Request for Comments (RFC)'s. IETF RFC 1122 provides the details of those capabilities. [5]

In broad terms, IP hosts should be hardened by steps such as the following to reduce or minimize the potential attack surface of the device.

- Change default device login information (login & password)
- Remove (or disable) any un-used applications and services
- Deleting guest or legacy user accounts
- Maintaining a proactive up to date patch or update routine
- Closing any device "backdoor" access
- Utilizing antivirus and malware protection with signature based deep packet inspection

- Backup of device data

Most computer-based devices found will be based upon the Microsoft Windows or a Linux operating system version. There is no absolute secure operating system as both platforms have potential vulnerabilities. Due to the different internal designs, an apples-to-apples comparison is not reasonable. Both can be made secure. Linux systems may offer more flexibility due to the open-source design. Windows is more of a closed system with limited flexibility. It should be noted that embedded versions of either operating system are commonly found in broadcast specific equipment found in the broadcast plant.

The growing popularity of Internet of Things (IoT) devices often create unique cybersecurity challenges. An IoT host device can be a variety of devices found in a modem broadcast facility. Common devices include security cameras, digital signage, thermostats, card access systems and even a light bulb. From a practical standpoint, these devices must be secured externally as they often lack basic security features due to limited or minimal operating system and cost. Due to limited resources (processor and memory), it is impossible to change defaults configurations or add cybersecurity protections such as antivirus and malware. Common practice is to place essential devices on their own subnet and utilize external packet filtering via an ACL and/or firewall to secure and control access.

Application cybersecurity protections are in general focused upon authentication and encryption of interaction between an individual user of the application and the application itself. Authentication is focused upon insuring the proper (known) user or application has the proper access and anyone else does not. Application security can be cumbersome, especially where multiple applications are involved. An authentication system is often referred to as a "single sign on" system and can be utilized to minimize the administrative tasks associated with application security. A major benefit allows the user access without the need to manage multiple login information. It is common for the system to provide federated identity techniques to secure application access and identification of the user or by another application. Two-factor authentication of users is often utilized as an added level of protection beyond simple login information exchange. In some cased, three-factor techniques can be applied to further add a protection barrier.

## Conclusions & Action Task Summary

The industry is well entranced in the vast array of "IP enabled" devices. No doubt the features provided are valuable to a broadcast facility and the convenience of the users. However, question whether every host device needs to be on the network or have public network access. If necessary, connect an essential device, then take the precautions to minimize the attack surface and a potential cybersecurity event.

An important consideration not addressed in this paper is network monitoring. Best practices in network management is monitoring to insure network operation in a proactive manner. Unusual network traffic patterns, unexplained increased in the use of resources can indicate that a cybersecurity incident is occurring. Knowing what is normal and alerting when it is not is an essential requirement of network and cybersecurity management.

This paper has attempted to present an overview of the cybersecurity threats likely to be faced, an overview of key cybersecurity practices that form best practices in the industry. A structured approach to implementation was presented that follows the data-flow layers of the OSI model structure. The design or the network or the architecture is the starting point for cybersecurity precaution. As a summary, in reality cybersecurity is a complex process. Figure 5 attempts to offer a simplified and focused checklist of implementable tasks for any network, large or small. These steps simply close opportunities and minimizes the attack surface risk presented to a potential attacker.

A final caution should be focused on your system users and social engineering techniques especially "phishing." As technology has improved to minimize cybersecurity, the use of phishing has significantly grown. It has grown because it has been effective. Phishing techniques exploit the human weakness of "wanting to be helpful." It is essential for your system users to be engaged and educated on the dangers of social engineering [6].

In summary, one cannot create or claim an absolute secure IT environment. However, you can take reasonable and implementable steps to minimize the attack surface of your IT infrastructure and to minimize the impact if a cybersecurity event should occur. Cybersecurity precautions require a balance between system use ability and security. Whereas there are cybersecurity best practices to offer guidance each situation is unique to the industry, organization and scope of the infrastructure environment. A single successful "phishing" attempt can instantly negate your cybersecurity efforts!

Yes, you can provide cybersecurity protection for your broadcast plant to minimize your risk of an incident. Be careful out there!

## Do These 12 Things

- Accept - Their is **NO SINGLE** Solution!
- Implement **multiple protections "DiD"**
- Change **default** logins
- Use **strong** passwords (paraphrases)
- **Separate** Admin & User accounts on hosts (WIN)
- **Segment** your network (VLAN) – reduce attack surface - create multi-layer security zones
- **Limit** access (users & applications) – apply "least privilege"
- Use packet **filtering** - control host access (ACL and/or firewall) – deny by default
- **Disable** un-used services – close ports not required
- Use **secure** access (SSH not telnet) & VPN for off-site access (2-factor authentication)
- **Monitor** you network – know what is normal
- Use "**intelligent**" host backup solutions – **test** backup restoration
- Keep systems **patched**
- Utilize **signature based** deep-packet inspection antivirus/malware – keep updated (often daily)
- Don't overlook **social engineering** – engage & educate users – **phishing** is alive and effective

FIGURE 5: ACTION TASK CHECKLIST.

## References

[1] National Institute of Standards and Technology Framework for Improving Critical Infrastructure Cybersecurity, v1.1, April 2018, https://www.nist.gov/cyberframework

[2] Santos, O., Muniz J., De Crescenzo, S., CCNA Cyber Ops Certification Guide, 2017, pp 162-163

[3] Fruhlinger, J., "The CIA triad: Definition, Components and Examples", CSOonline.com, 2/10/2020.

[4] Harwood, M., CompTIA Network+, 2009, pp. 134-135

[5] Braden, R., Internet Engineering Task Force, RFC 1122, October 1989, pp. 108-111

[6] Federal Trade Commission, Cybersecurity for Small Business - Phishing, https://www.ftc.gov/tips-advice/business-center/small-businesses/cybersecurity/phishing

# Cyber Hygiene
# Protecting Content in a Work-From-Home Environment

**Gary Olson**
**GHO Group LLC**
**New York, New York, United States**
gary@ghogroup.com

**Abstract** – The global pandemic changed the way people worked driving a massive Work from Home (WFH) initiative and creating new challenges in the entire media supply chain. Telecommuting and @Home became Work-From-Home, and Cyber Security (technology) and Cyber Hygiene (Best Practices) became critical considerations to support this new operating environment.

The transition to IP and computer-based technology in media production requires new considerations that include cyber protection. Vendors and service providers need to support cybersecurity in their products and services and users (production personnel, technicians, and operators) need to follow a new set of guidelines for best cybersecurity practices or "Cyber Hygiene."

Super Bowl LV had over 300 remote operators using their home internet service and home computers. While the exposure and opportunity for a problem was mind-numbing, fortunately there were no reported incidents, and everyone was onboard with paying attention.

In WFH, the use of home wireless is the most common and probably an unsecure connection. Now if we consider all the new connected devices (IoT or the Insecurity of Things) that have become prevalent, and this exponentially increases the potential for a cyber-attack. Making sure there are good secure and reliable connections is only the first part of Work from Home challenges. Keeping content safe, preventing corruption, and protecting the remote access production systems are critical considerations and requirements for security teams.

There are a number of cyber security products, technologies and protocols available. Typically corporations and enterprises (Broadcasters, Leagues, etc.) specify the security products they use and will support. They also have Cyber Security rules and policies that govern on premise and secure remote connections. Although they were already working on Bring Your Own Device (BYOD) strategies, when the pandemic struck and BYOD changed to WFH.

In the world of WFH, organizations don't have the "control" over the user's endpoint device and what, if any, security precautions or products the WFH user might or might not be using. Since these users use their own devices, how they are configured is largely ungoverned. This makes it even more important to have good Cyber Hygiene aka the best security practices and guidelines.

This paper will outline some of the issues, concerns, and challenges, and present for consideration some best-practice guidelines without specific product references.

This paper is excerpted from the Proceedings of the 2021 NAB Broadcast Engineering and Information Technology (BEIT) Conference, 

## Introduction

There have been a number of recent very public cyber-attacks that have caused considerable damage and disrupted critical operations and services at a very high cost. While the hackers have been given a lot of credit for their sophistication, in reality the actual intrusions were not sophisticated at all. Once they gained access, they then applied very sophisticated technology to cause destructive damage to an extent that it is still largely unknown how extensive the damage or potential for disruption actually is.

The Solarwinds compromise was traced back to an intern (many years ago) given the responsibility to create the MASTER administrative password for Solarwinds products. The intern left after a year and posted the password online – undetected. Over the years, no one found it necessary to change or update the master password and recently a bad actor found it online and the rest as we say is history. One of the unspoken realities of the Solarwinds incident is how far reaching the impact is. It's more that the Solarwinds customer bases. Networks interconnect with each other independent of manufacturer, protocols or management systems. This means that any "infected" network can easily "infect" another one. That translates to mobile units, broadcast centers, and production and distribution centers. Other incidents like the Florida water issue, Colonial Pipeline and meat processing plant ransomware attacks were traced back to open remote access applications that created the connection used by WFH operators – OOPS.

This is where ***Cyber Hygiene*** and best practices become important. Cyber protection and safety are only effective when the users understand how important it is to practice good cyber hygiene.

The broadcast industry needs to work closely with the IT security community, and the broadcast technology community needs to adopt best practices in their products, services, and operations.

### Challenges

Case Study*: The mobile production industry was one of the early media businesses to begin production during COVID. Even before COVID, many in the freelance production community did prep work at home and then brought graphics, text, clips, and device configurations (switcher setups) to the remote production mobile unit typically on their personal removable media. The same media device stores family pictures, shopping information, maybe reading materials and potentially a virus or ransomware. During a world champion sporting event and shortly before airtime, a manufacturer's tech showed up with a service patch on a flash drive, insisted on doing the patch and infected the production switcher - coming very close to preventing the event from going live.*

Another challenge is the wild - wild world of Internet connections, the most obvious being public vs private internet access. It's likely that most WFH users use Wi-Fi connectivity in their home. Unfortunately, what's also connected to the Wi-Fi are all the IoT devices such as Alexa/Siri, baby monitors, doorbells, home security and smart devices i.e. TV, InstaPot, etc. Additionally, people want their phones to access and control all these devices remotely, which means they are accessible from the outside via some full-time connected app. This exposes the home Internet service to possibly becoming compromised.

A common situation is when users keep multiple browser tabs open and use common logins or stay logged in to multiple websites. Even if a VPN is used for remote access to production, if there are social media sites, shopping sites and web based email accounts open at the same time, all of these communicate with each other and can provide full access to the protected connection. Another security risk is uploading files to a cloud service without first scanning them. The first user to download it unsuspectingly may bring a virus or ransomware to the remote connection and infect other endpoints.

Remote connection applications (i.e. Team Viewer, VNC, LogMeIn, and PCAnywhere) are widely used to enable access and control to a remote device. These typically use a cloud intermediary service, which opens the possibility for a bad actor to access the remote device. Users share the ID and password in email or leave it as a default. Some of the remote access products do not truly end the session or disrupt the connection once the session is ended. This leaves the onsite device exposed to entry (Florida water supply event).

### Cyber Hygiene

Cyber security typically refers to various software and hardware technologies. These are anti-virus, anti-malware, firewalls, intrusion detection and others. Cyber Hygiene refers to following some basic principles, guidelines and best practices to improve the chances of preventing intrusion, infection and disruption and to insure good cyber health.

As a result of the mobile unit use case study above, the mobile truck industry came together and formed an advisory group. We created a set of recommendations that could be adopted by all the mobile truck vendors, broadcasters and leagues. One of the first guidelines we introduced to the community was to have an "air gapped" computer for scanning for personal drives and requiring that any removable media brought onto the mobile unit MUST be scanned. This air gapped device is a standalone computer, not attached to the Internet, internal network or any other device, this computer is running multiple virus/malware scanning services and only gets connected to the Internet for updating virus definitions. If any removable media fails, it is not allowed to be used on any device in the truck. Another recommendation is to have a separate "guest" Wi-Fi network that is fully isolated from the production Wi-Fi network, that people could use for their personal email and other activities. This protects the mission critical Wi-Fi network that production services need for operations.

The WFH challenges come from a number of typical user practices. Many web services and mobile apps provide single sign-on capability using the same username and password from one of the popular social media services, i.e. LinkedIn, Facebook or Google. This means that once a browser is open it's likely that all services are automatically logged in. With mobile apps, once a user allows the app to log in using the device account, it maintains a full-time open connection. Another challenge is the ever present "accept cookies" waiver that is now prevalent. It does not state "only for this session" which means that even though the user closes the browser, the history, data and tracking cookies are very active.

IoT adds another layer of insecurity. In the home, the number of connected devices continues to grow exponentially. One of the recent security concerns is the Amazon Sidewalk project, where Amazon is essentially creating a mesh network, sharing a user's Wi-Fi using its home personal assistant devices across an entire neighborhood of users. This provides Amazon unregulated access to all IoT devices across entire neighborhoods and communities.

WFH remote production can involve remote access to a live production device such as instant replay or graphics or remote creative such as meltdowns or sizzles and file transfer for pre/post-production work. For live events, controlling live devices requires a latency free reliable connection. While this presents multiple challenges, this paper focuses on the WFH environment.

How many home IoT devices can be accessed via an app remotely? Security systems, digital assistants, home monitoring? How many of these are either unprotected or using default names? All these easily expose the home network to being compromised. Here are some basic questions to ask:

- Is the network password protected with something other than the default that came with the router?
- Does the router have a firewall setting and is it on?

There are very real concerns in deploying and supporting WFH production and its ability for a remote operator to compromise a live production by using an open, unprotected connection or by submitting corrupt content uploaded for contribution or distribution. On a recent cyber security call, one of the security executives of a major station group mentioned his team discovered ransomware in a media file that was uploaded to an internal FTP site for program distribution. It's likely whoever was uploading the file did not know their system was comprised. The next question is how can the content be replaced in time for air if the individual producing it has a compromised system?

### Guidelines

There are some basic best practices that may be less convenient than using autofill for passwords, or shopping while operating an instant replay device or graphics system.

1. Set web browsers to clear history, cookies and data on exit.
2. Do not open a browser session if the remote connection does not require it.
3. Limit the number of open browser windows and tabs to essential portals for remote operations.
4. Scan all media files, scripts and device configurations for viruses and malware BEFORE connecting to the remote system.
    a. Use an air-gapped computer as the DMZ for downloading any type of file and scanning it prior to placing it into an active production system.
    b. Keep the virus and malware applications, and definitions, current at all times.
5. Separate removable media devices for personal and work-related content.
    a. Do not use flash drives with personal content for production related files
    b. Scan removable drives before introducing them into mission critical production equipment.
6. Where possible use a wired (Ethernet) connection.
    a. This only removes the Wi-Fi exposure
7. Cyber protection
    a. Router firewall
    b. Virus software
    c. Malware software

One of the more difficult challenges is separating the computer used for remote production from the home IoT devices and other people sharing the same home Wi-Fi network.

The National Institute for Science and Technology (NIST) has published a pretty extensive set of recommended rules, policies and guidelines for good cyber health, called the NIST Cybersecurity Framework. This may be a bit onerous for a WFH operator/technician, but it provides good information for an organization's cyber security team. EBU has published a set of recommendations to manufacturers and vendors regarding cyber safeguards and some best practices for their products and services.

Good cyber hygiene helps maintain good cyber health and good cyber health keeps systems and devices protected and operating.

The bad guys are working very hard to disrupt things and WFH introduced a new layer of opportunity to them. It's up to the WFH people to participate by helping to cyber protect themselves and any remote production they are involved with.

## References

[1] The National Institute for Science and Technology (NIST) - Cybersecurity Framework Version 1.1 https://www.nist.gov/cyberframework/framework

[2] European Broadcast Union - Recommendation - EBU R143 - Cybersecurity for media vendor systems, software & services - https://tech.ebu.ch/publications/r143

# Living with Current Faults at End-of-Branch Broadcast Facilities


**Thomas LaBarge, John Broccoli, Nancy Swartz, John H. Belk**
**Groundlinx Technologies**
**Blue Ridge, Georgia, United States**
info@groundlinx.com



**Abstract** – Broadcast facilities are subject to numerous current and power faults from myriad sources including those related to power generation and transmission. Lightning strikes are of course an additional notable source of risk to proper electrical function of facilities whether the result of a strike, a local current surge, electrical noise on power lines from a distant strike, or switching-related power outages. Any of these current faults can result in the need for repairs and down time which adds to expenses and business risk. We have observed that being located at the far end of an electrical branch, often located thousands of feet down the line from its nearest neighbors, may put a broadcast facility at increased risk. Technical and business risks to an end-of-branch broadcast facility can be mitigated in part by acting on an improved understanding of the broadband nature of the energy in such faults.


While analyzing broadcast facility grounding systems, the authors have noted that disruptive current-related incidents seem to occur more often at the end of power line branches. These facilities are often relatively distant from any other facilities. Positioning a broadcast (or any other) facility at the end of an electrical branch would appear to put it at increased uptime risk. This typically correlates with the facility also being at the far end of a power line distribution branch but the same could be true for a transmission branch. See Figure 1.

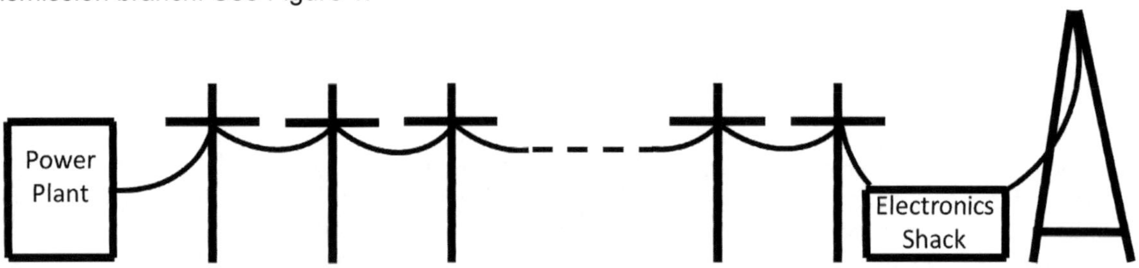


FIGURE 1: BROADCAST FACILITY FAR FROM ITS UTILITY POWER PLANT.

While standard utility company grounding is often sufficient for the energies and frequencies commonly found in low energy surges and spikes, higher energy spikes from major switchgear faults and lightning strikes can overwhelm common utility grounding even when the incoming branch grounding is relatively intact. Unattenuated faults may reach structures and equipment whenever shelter or tower grounding is insufficient. This means that local structures as well as power lines can act as conduits for large fault currents into the building and its electronics package. This needs to be part of any facility's overall grounding strategy.


This paper is excerpted from the Proceedings of the 2021 NAB Broadcast Engineering and Information Technology (BEIT) Conference, © 2021, National Association of Broadcasters, 1 M Street S.E., Washington, DC 20003 USA.

## Causes

There are many possible causes for the anecdotal data that led the authors to seek to understand if indeed their developing hypothesis that branch ends are more susceptible to damage is accurate and, if so, how to combat the situation.

### Cause: Out of Sight, Out of Mind

The public's aversion to the sight of towers and a reduced cost of land far from town may play a part in a facility's being located quite remotely, of course, but during emergencies (e.g., weather-related) a location so far from other customers can reduce the chance of getting serviced as compared to facilities located in more densely populated areas within a power company's service area. For example, a storm passes through an area and the accompanying lighting strikes cause power outages as do the storms themselves with water flow and flooding. The affected power company may get busy accommodating the needs of its customers where they are, generally near town, not out in remote locations. This is understandable as the power supplier is generally focused on reducing the number of customers struggling without service as fast as they can while hoping to keep their uptimes intact. An unattended radio tower outside town is not going to be first priority unless the facility houses International Building Code Structure Class III and Class IV towers or towers which are similarly responsible for essential communications.

### Cause: Length of the Branch

It appears that the farther a broadcast facility is from its power generation plant, the more opportunities there are for faults along the way, lightning or otherwise, to disrupt its power quality. One significant contributor to fault current making it to the end of the branch (and a nearby broadcast facility) is the quality and condition of both the pole grounds and transformer grounds along the branch. A long incoming string of poorly grounded power poles reduces draining of fault currents and can damage the reliability of broadcast facility function considerably. While electric utility pole grounding may be generally sufficient for normal operations, it is very possibly inadequate for extreme or high energy surges, even those much less disruptive faults than lightning strikes. If the overall protection of the broadcast facility relies on proper grounding of multiple transformers along the branch and some of these grounding locations are compromised, the broadcast facility is at increased risk from any fault coming down that branch.

### Cause: Soil Electrical Properties and Corrosion

Our measurements of power pole grounds have often been quite disappointing whether the installer simply installed a couple grounds rods at a new installation, perhaps without verifying resistance-to-ground (RTG) in that soil, or when the utility company just has not replaced or maintained their ground rods consistently. RTGs of over 700 Ohms have been common in our experience with measurements of greater than 1,000 Ohms discovered. See Figure 2. Many grids globally need refurbishment in part due to age but also to improve reliability and increase functionality so that they can accommodate new grid elements that are required for a reliable and flexible transmission grid.

FIGURE 2: RTG 700 OHMS, FAR HIGHER THAN THE US NEC CODE LIMIT OF 25 OHMS.

Resistances in parallel, like found in a branch containing a series of utility poles, add as their inverses which means that in a long string, the loss of a few electrical grounds anywhere along a branch could well be tolerable, at least theoretically. One has to only remember that there is also a good chance that if a few have corroded, so have many, many more as they're all located in one region and likely similar soil. And if the soil is poor for electrical grounding (high RTGs), like that in Figure 2, it takes many, many ground rods to approach NEC standards. As a consequence, the poorer the electrical properties of the soil, the lower the percentage of a branch's ground rods it would take to severely damage the grounding capability of a branch putting the broadcast facility at risk.

### Cause: Renewable Power

Changes in the power generation market are also raising risk for the lonely broadcast facility. These sites are getting assaulted with changing power generation source current quality as renewables like wind and solar power come online. Renewably generated current generally fluctuates more than that from conventional generation. While renewable power can increase reliability and flexibility of the new grid, variations in output due to clouds and changing winds can reduce reliability and flexibility of the grid's infrastructure. In addition to these simple fluctuations, as renewables rise in prominence, there will be insufficient nearby rotating mass generators in the system to provide frequency stability whenever a large load rejection or addition occurs on the grid.

## High Frequency Considerations

Any fault with a rapid onset or fall-off will have higher frequencies. Lightning, for example, has components far into the MHz and even into the GHz, with a relatively major spike around 60 MHz. Copper's electrical conductivity declines as frequencies rise while the current carrying capability of a wire or ribbon also gets smaller as frequencies increase (due to skin depth) so it does not take as much energy at high frequencies to do damage as it would at low frequencies. Lighting's voltage and current can exceed 250 kV and 30 kA respectively and its components at higher frequencies can behave differently than at the typical 50-60 Hz we normally deal with.

When a bolt of lightning arrives with its *very* rapid current increase, it is accompanied by large amount of current at low and high frequencies. The high frequency portion of this pulse passes preferentially through the surfaces of your conductors (wires, cables, buss bars, ribbons) while the charge current chooses its path. By virtue of frequency's effect on skin depth, these currents exist preferentially on the surface of the conductors where they are ready and able to arc to nearby conductors (wires, tower legs, rebar, etc.) It is crucial to attenuate as much of these high frequencies as possible as soon as possible while simultaneously maintaining enough capacity to absorb the rest of the lightning strike's onslaught of broadband current. And this must be done for faults coming into the broadcast system facility from both external (utility power, communication lines) and internal sources (e.g., lighting strikes the transmission tower, internal electrical faults, etc.).

## Risk Reduction

The branch-end broadcast facility operator's first choice would be for their utility company to not deliver current faults to their broadcast facility at all or to not deliver power without its faults being suitably attenuated along the way. However, if the utility companies are unable to quickly upgrade their grounding systems for their incoming delivery systems, solutions must be considered which address these concerns within the physical land and property of the broadcast facility itself. This means that the broadcast facility itself would be required to dissipate a large amount of fault current coming down utility wires with large and sharp transients from lightning strikes and switchgear faults to accommodate compromised utility company delivery systems. Large capacity and efficient broadband dissipation would be the goal to increase the end-of-branch facility's uptime and decrease its annual repair and replacement costs.

## Summary

The end-of-branch broadcast facility often exhibits a nearly perfect storm of risks and an outsized amount of damage and related downtime and expenses. Out on the edge of town, stuck with poorly grounded incoming utility power, staring at higher odds for suffering current faults along the utility branch delivering its power, the broadcast facility is trying in vain to live within the limits of its power utility's aging infrastructure. While the power utility industry offers insufficiently installed or maintained grounding infrastructure, the broadcast industry cannot be properly prepared for the rapid arrival of 5G and other higher frequencies systems, especially at end-of-branch broadcast facilities and especially considering lightning strikes, without installing some of its own onsite protection.

# 8K JPEG XS Codec Adapted to SMPTE ST 2110

**Kota Itakura, Masayuki Miyazaki**
**Japan Broadcasting Corporation (NHK)**
**Tokyo, Japan**
itakura.k-fy@nhk.or.jp, miyazaki.m-fw@nhk.or.jp

**Michael Van Dorpe**
**Village Island Co., Ltd.**
**Tokyo, Japan**
m-vandorpe@village-island.com

**Abstract** – NHK developed an 8K interface device using JPEG XS corresponding to SMPTE ST 2110. Thus far, we have used quad-linked 12G-SDI or bundled 4K-IP interfaces for interfacing 8K production devices. However, the cable counts tended to increase, the production systems became complex, and the facilitation cost increased. Furthermore, a problem arose due to an increase in the power consumption of the system resulting from an increase in the number of gateways. JPEG XS is a light-weight codec attracting considerable attention among the broadcasters worldwide owing to its high coding efficiency, high picture quality, and low latency. We expect that it can be registered to the SMPTE ST 2110 family. Although HD or 4K devices are presently available in the market, no 8K JPEG XS codec has yet been developed. After prototyping a software-based 8K codec using a current PC in 2019, we presented it at the IBC 2020 and SMPTE 2020 and attracted the interest of a broad audience. Using the prototype, we derived the optimum compression ratio for an 8K program production through quality evaluation. In 2020, we developed the ST 2110-compliant 8K JPEG XS codec, which has a compression and an IP processing unit implemented on an FPGA (Field Programmable Gate Array). It can transmit two 8K streams over a relatively inexpensive 10 GbE (Giga-bit Ethernet) interface with ultra-low latency while maintaining a high image quality, which can greatly contribute to the commoditization of 8K production systems. In parallel, aiming for miniaturization, we designed it so that two codecs can be installed in a 1RU chassis. In this paper, we introduce our development and refer to the system design when introducing it to an 8K production facility. We have been developing an interface for 8K productions to easily manage immense 8K streaming via a single interface. Finally, we developed an IP interface adopting JPEG XS compression and SMPTE ST 2110. This paper introduces our development process.

## Introduction

NHK started research on 8K Super Hi-Vision in 1995. The production of 8K programs has been on the rise since 2010, when the development of practical production equipment progressed. However, we used a non-standard video format called DG (dual green). This method utilizes the elemental technologies of HD production while aligning with the imaging format of cameras that employ pixel shifting technologies. In recent years, there has been a shift to the 4:2:2 color sampling method, which is highly compatible with the 4K technology that is evolving along with 8K. The technology that uses four 12G-SDI interfaces (4K Quad Link) has become an international standard and is the current mainstream 8K production format (Figure 1). In parallel, solutions using IP technologies have also

This paper is excerpted from the Proceedings of the 2021 NAB Broadcast Engineering and Information Technology (BEIT) Conference, © 2021, National Association of Broadcasters, 1 M Street S.E., Washington, DC 20003 USA.

begun to appear in the broadcasting industry, and technology to bundle four 4K IP signals has been partially introduced in 8K OB-vans or studio systems.

Notably, the 8K production technology continues to evolve, but all methods require multiple interfaces and cables to transmit a single 8 K video/audio stream. This has increased the scale, cost, and power consumption of the equipment, and the need to secure a large installation space and powerful air-conditioning capacity—which is currently vital especially in OB-VAN situations for 8K productions; this has been one of the factors preventing the commoditization of 8K production equipment.

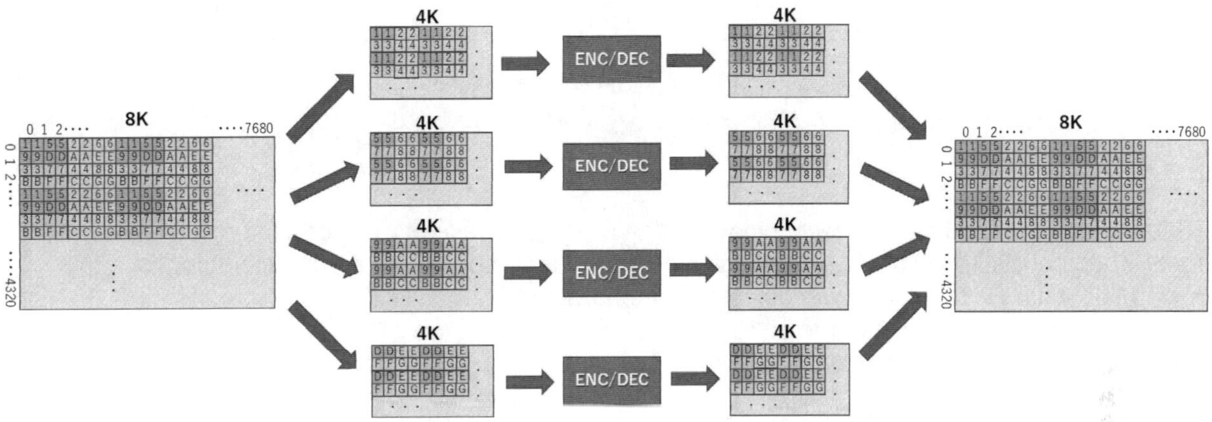


FIGURE 1: 8K VIDEO (4:2:2 SAMPLING) TRANSPORTATION WITH 4K QUAD LINK

## Development Purpose

In developing this system, we focused on the IP interface, which is becoming increasingly popular worldwide owing to the expansion of the network market and is expected to have a large capacity. We developed this system to reduce the scale of the equipment by transmitting 8K signals (4:2:2 sampling/10bit/59.94p) via a single physical interface and to adapt it to future transmission methods within and from outside the broadcasting station.

To efficiently transmit large amounts of 8K video information exceeding 40 Gbps, it is essential to introduce compression technologies; therefore, JPEG XS, a compression method suitable for production, was adopted based on the features described in the following section. Figure 2 shows the developed codec device, and Table 1 lists the specifications.

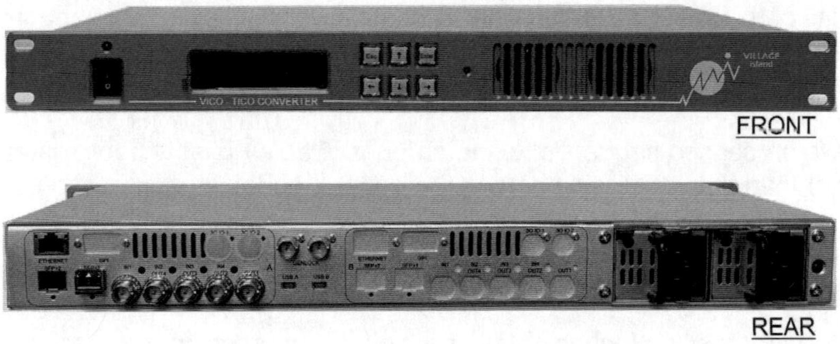


FIGURE 2: DEVELOPED IP INTERFACE DEVICE

| | |
|---|---|
| SIZE | 432(W) x 262(D) x 44(H) |
| INPUT / OUTPUT PORT | 4 x BNC (SMPTE ST 2082-12)<br>2 x SFP+ (SMPTE ST 2110)<br>2 x BNC (GENLOCK and LOOP THROUGH)<br>1 x RJ45 (MAINTENANCE) |
| POWER | Max. 70W |
| VIDEO FORMAT | 7680 x 4320, 59.94p, 4:2:2, 10bit |
| NUMBER OF AUDIO CHANNEL | 32ch |

TABLE 1: SPEC SHEET

## JPEG XS

JPEG XS is a light compression technology that performs the wavelet transform in units of slices (a strip of video consisting of 16 lines), as shown in Figure 3, and has the following advantages:

- Maintaining video quality without visual deterioration
- Less computation, lighter processing
- Resistance to repeated compression
- Minimal latency
- Specification is public and can be used as an open format

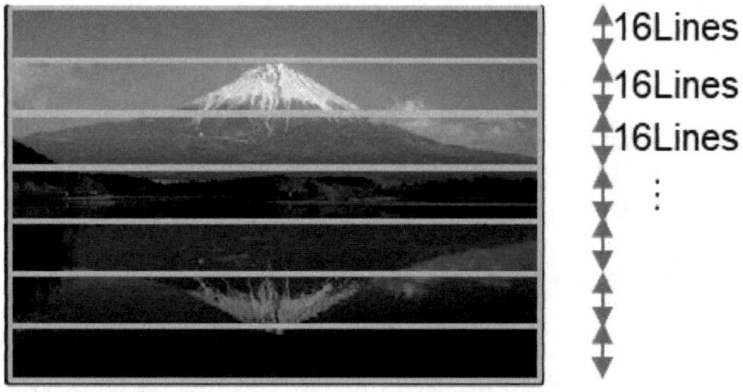


FIGURE 3: JPEG XS SLICE UNITS

In 8K productions, where an ultra-high definition is the most important feature, it is especially important to maintain the quality of the images created on the location during the subsequent process. JPEG XS is visually indistinguishable from the degradation of the compression ratio up to a certain level and can maintain a high level of image quality before encoding.

Because each slice is processed sequentially, the amount of delay is only approximately a dozen lines, which is much shorter than the processing time of the general codecs that process each frame.

## Picture Quality Evaluation

In general, with video compression technologies, the higher compression ratio results in a greater amount of data that can be reduced; however, the picture quality simultaneously decreases. While considering the adoption of the 8K JPEG XS, it was necessary to derive the optimal compression ratio for the production.

To ensure the possibility of changing the compression ratio, as a first step, a prototype codec was created in the software, and an objective evaluation was conducted using ARIB's 8K standard video images. Meanwhile, to conduct subjective evaluations using the videos, we emphasized on the ability to encode and decode the prototype in real time.

For the objective evaluation, the image quality was compared using only Link A from the Quad Link for both the original and decoded video using a 4K measurement device. Moreover, because the 8K image was evaluated using a 4K image divided by 2SI 2-sample interleave (SI), it was assumed that the measurement values could be equivalent to the entire 8K image (Figure 4). Some of these results are presented in Table 2.

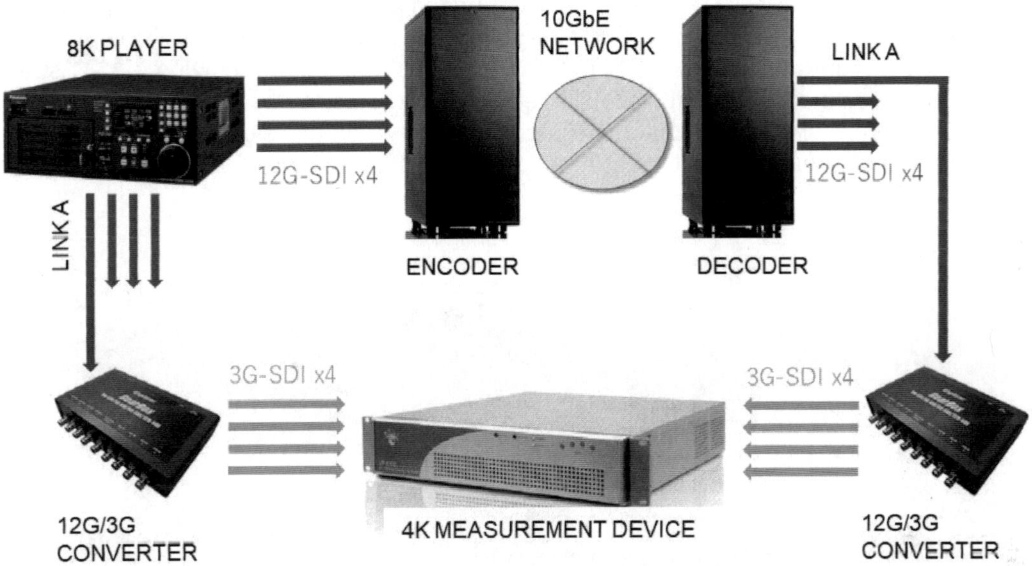


FIGURE 4: OBJECTIVE EVALUATION SYSTEM

| | Peak Signal-to-Noise Ratio (dB) | | | | |
|---|---|---|---|---|---|
| Comp. Ratio | Maiko  | Train  | Maple 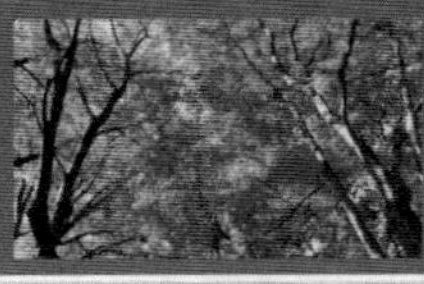 | River  | Rate (Gbps) |
| 8:1 | 52.25 | 50.44 | 41.39 | 40.30 | 5.19 |
| 10:1 | 51.03 | 49.32 | 39.81 | 37.84 | 3.87 |
| 12:1 | 50.13 | 48.28 | 38.46 | 36.38 | 3.24 |
| 16:1 | 49.12 | 47.01 | 36.63 | 34.00 | 2.60 |

TABLE 2: OBJECTIVE EVALUATION RESULTS (EXCERPT)

In general, if the error is distributed over the entire screen, and the peak signal-to-noise ratio (PSNR) is 40 dB or more, it is evaluated as "visually lossless," where no difference can be recognized visually. Among the evaluated images in Table 2, "Maiko" and "Train" are normal images in terms of compression processing difficulty, whereas "Maple" and "River" are complex images that contain many high-frequency components and extreme luminance components and are known in various compression technologies as images with high compression processing difficulty. In the case of an 8:1 compression, all images showed a PSNR of 40 dB or higher. Regarding the JPEG XS, an 8:1 compression can be evaluated as a practical codec for production.

## Recommended Compression Ratio For 8K Production

In IP multicast transmission, when switching videos, video switching cannot be performed by blanking switching methods such as serial digital interface (SDI)-based baseband signals, but by receiving and controlling IP streams. The stream control image for achieving shock-free video switching (clean switching) is shown in Figure 5. When switching the image on the monitor receiving the C1 stream to C2, the receiver receives the C2 stream while still receiving the C1 stream, displays the C2 image, and then stops the C1 stream. This means that there are moments when two signals are temporarily flowing; therefore, to achieve clean switching, a bandwidth of at least twice the video bit rate is required in the transmission channel.

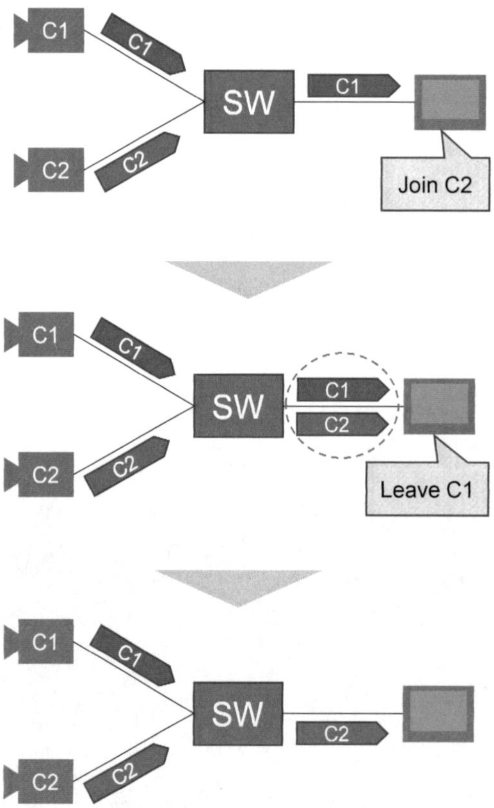


FIGURE 5: CLEAN SWITCHING (C1 TO C2)

As shown in the rightmost column of Table 2, an 8:1 compression requires a bandwidth of 5.19 Gbps. When 10GbE products and lines are used, an 8:1 compression cannot provide twice the bandwidth, and packet loss occurs every time a video is switched. A method of packet shaping by adding a buffer at the transmission end is also considered, but it is difficult to adopt in production facilities because of the increased latency. In the case of a 10:1 compression, it is 3.87 Gbps per stream, which means that clean switching can be achieved even with 10GbE. In a 10:1 compression, the PSNR is slightly below 40 dB for the "Maple" and "River" images, but as mentioned above, these two images are exceptions to the high degree of difficulty in compression processing. Further, a concern arises in that if the image quality and bit rate are specified for these images, they could be over-specified for many other images.

Therefore, we conducted a subjective evaluation using video for each 10:1 compressed image. As a result, it was confirmed that even with a 10:1 compression, there was almost no perceptible degradation in the video and no problem with the image quality, thus the recommended compression ratio for the 8K JPEG XS in program production was derived as 10:1.

## Hardware Version Development

Having confirmed the usefulness of the JPEG XS and IP interfaces with the trial software, the next step was to develop hardware products for field use. In addition to implementing the JPEG XS compression algorithm and IP packetization processing in an FPGA, the system is also capable of transmitting audio and ANC data multiplexed on four 12G SDI systems, which are the input interfaces of the codec device. Implemented in a hardware, the compression process is faster, with a latency of less than 1 ms from the encoder input to the decoder output.

In addition, the newly developed devices can operate as either an encoder or a decoder by switching the operation mode. This allows for flexibility depending on the site of the operation and is also expected to reduce the costs through mass production.

A picture of the device is shown in Figure 6. All processing can be integrated into a board size of less than half the size of a single 1U chassis, and it is possible to implement two codecs in the same chassis. Because the JPEG XS requires less computation for compression processing, it is suitable for compact implementations, and we believe that in the future, it will be possible to implement it in the interface part of cameras, recording equipment, video switchers, etc.

FIGURE 6: DEVICE INTERIOR

## Conclusion

We began developing this project in 2018, and by converting it into hardware after sufficient verification, we were able to achieve our goal of handling 8K signals with a single interface. In addition, by adapting to SMPTE ST 2110, which is now being introduced, and designing the system to allow the use of low-cost 10GbE networks, we believe that we can reduce the cost of the production systems such as studios and OB-vans, and expand into remote production. We will continue to develop technologies that will make 8K production more common and easier to work with and contribute to the development of broadcasting technology.

# Distributing and Synchronizing Signals Between the Worlds of SDI and IP

**Renaud Lavoie, Sithideth Viengkhou,**
**Sebastien Berthiaume, Daniel Tremblay**
**Riedel Communications GmbH & Co. KG**
**Wuppertal, Germany**

**Abstract** – Moving signals between the worlds of SDI and IP isn't exactly rocket science, but synchronizing these signals may prove to be a challenge. It is these cases that we will discuss in this paper and these challenges that we seek to identify and present a viable and cost-effective solution to.

For this paper, we will consider a recent Riedel project with a major US broadcaster. Following the decision to move its operations to ST 2110, the broadcast network experienced synchronization problems between its IP-based flagship station and more than 200 affiliate stations throughout North America relying on SDI. The fact that the remote feeds needed to be compressed posed yet another challenge, as it required the decompressed signal to be decoded to ST 2110 before they could be converted to SDI.

The Riedel team managed to solve the synchronization issue with a single, powerful device smaller than the size of your thumb: A software-defined processing small form-factor pluggable (SFP) which enabled the conversion of UHD and ST 2110 signals for bidirectional distribution between the headquarters and the affiliate stations while generating a PTP Grand Master clock from the affiliate's synchronized signal. This greatly reduced both system complexity and the cost of replacing the entire affiliate synchronization system.

After a general description of the specific use case setup, this paper presents an overview of the various possible solutions and weighs the pros and cons before focusing on the most viable solution. After short explanations of the demarcation switch configuration and the Epoch reference generation at the affiliate sites, this document concludes with an outlook on other potential use cases.

## Use Case Description

As stated in the abstract, the Riedel team was tasked with assisting a major broadcast network with its move to ST 2110. The key challenge was to synchronize the flagship station IP signals with the SDI signals of the affiliate stations across North America. These SDI signals were clock-locked, and phase-aligned with the local Black Burst SPG, but with no timing relation to the flagship station IP feeds.

In this particular use case, the feeds coming from the flagship station are sent over H.264/H.265. The decoder of the incoming stream provides ST 2110 signals in the demarcation switches at the affiliate sites. This is where the problems come in because the ST 2110 stream is free-running, as opposed to the station's Black Burst.

This paper is excerpted from the Proceedings of the 2021 NAB Broadcast Engineering and Information Technology (BEIT) Conference, © 2021, National Association of Broadcasters, 1 M Street S.E., Washington, DC 20003 USA.

Finding a solution that would satisfy all stakeholders was no easy feat, as both budgets and technological conditions varied greatly between affiliate stations in different regions. Many remote sites or studios were equipped with sync pulse generators (SPG) without PTP Grand Master capabilities, turning any solution that would require affiliates to change their SPG into a substantial investment.

To provide a PTP reference without forcing all affiliates to change their SPG, the Riedel team proposed a solution that included a Grand Master Add-On installed on a software-defined SFP. Equipped with this software, the SFP can act as an encapsulator to send 12G-SDI UHD video over ST 2110 while generating a PTP Grand Master based on the vertical blanking interval (VBI) of the affiliates.

## Possible Solutions

As the following images show, there were four possible solutions:

(1) One was to change the SPGs at all of the affiliate facilities.

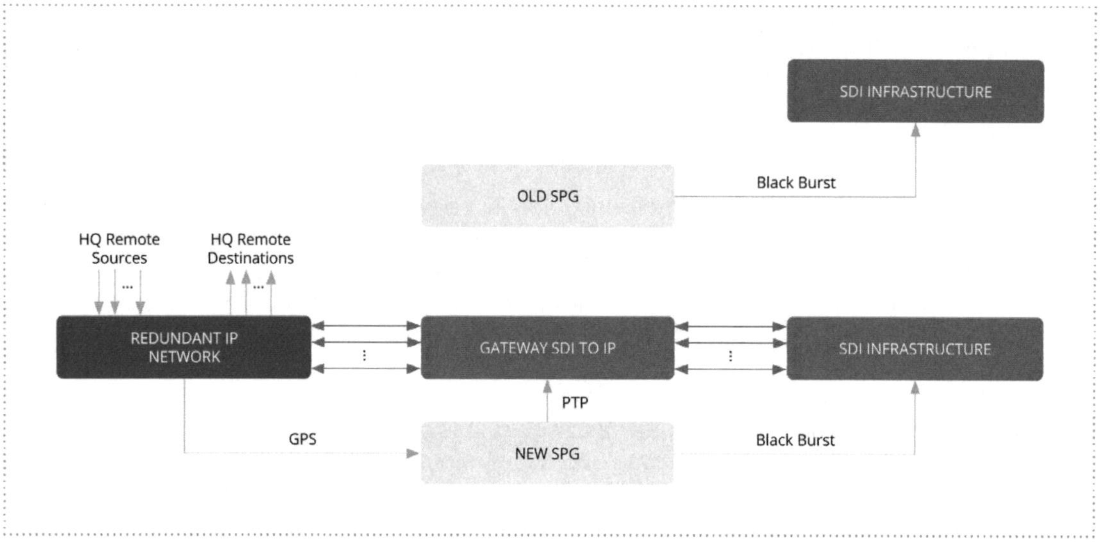


FIGURE 1. SOLUTION 1: UPGRADING ALL SPGS

Upgrading all SPGs and priming them for full-IP environments would certainly bring some advantages, but the costs would be unmanageable due to the sheer number of stations (about 200 affiliate stations).

(2) Another option was to synchronize all the affiliates to the flagship station via PTP.

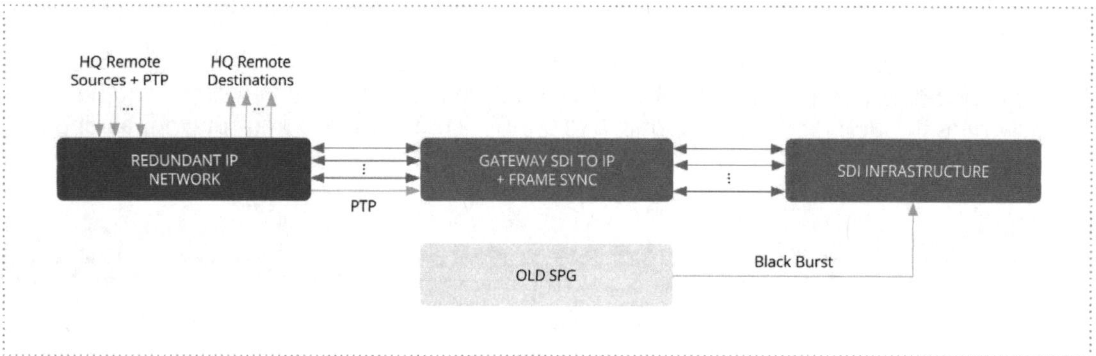


FIGURE 2. SOLUTION 2: SYNCHRONIZING ALL THE AFFILIATES TO HQ VIA PTP

This approach simply was not feasible because of the compression format and the architecture of the connection between HQ and the affiliates. While this solution would have its merits, as all affiliates would have been synchronized on one GPS, bandwidth limitations made this practically impossible. Another negative aspect would be the lack of PTP redundancy.

(3) A third approach was to add frame synchronizers on the de-encapsulators and to any equipment bridging the ST 2110 streams to and from the station.

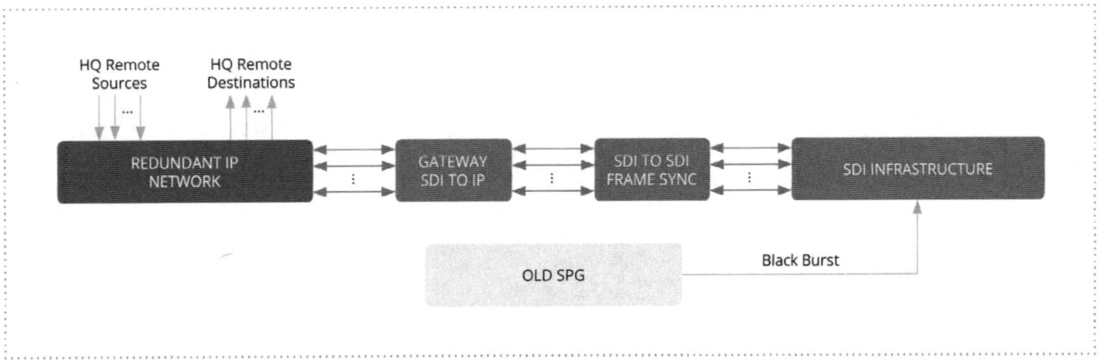


FIGURE 3. SOLUTION 3: ADDING FRAME SYNCHRONIZERS

This would not be a good long-term investment, as the frame synchronizers in the affiliate stations would become obsolete once the affiliates fully move to ST 2110. And apart from being a waste of resources, space, and power, this solution lacks a PTP master presence for third-party ST 2110 equipment and would also introduce additional points of failure.

(4) The fourth option involved the software-defined SFPs. This solution stood out because it involved no additional hardware cost; instead, the network would purchase software licenses only where needed. The gateways were necessary to achieve the IP to SDI transmission anyway, and if a station already had an SPG for SDI (without GPS) with Grand Master functionality, it would not even have to buy the add-on.

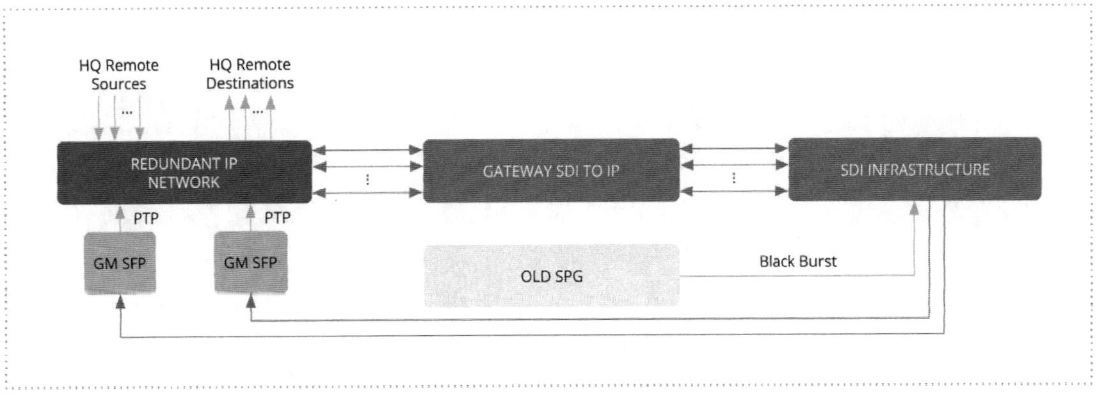


FIGURE 4. SOLUTION 4: THE MUON B GRAND MASTER ADD-ON

After considering all options, the customer opted for the SFP solution. Besides reduced cost and effort, the ability to encapsulate and generate Grand Master signals with a single device was a key decision driver.

## Implementation

The customer needed the ability to send multiple feeds from the head office to all of the affiliate stations and also receive return feeds from the affiliates. Initially, the signals were supposed to be sent uncompressed via ST 2110, but due to bandwidth cost over the long distance, it was decided to compress the video, audio, and ancillary data to minimize the required bandwidth.

Therefore, WAN encoders/decoders were set up at the affiliate stations to take in the compressed streams and convert them to ST 2110, which could then be de-encapsulated to SDI by advanced SFP gateways. The SDI to IP gateways also enable the affiliates to encapsulate their SDI signals to ST 2110 and then send compressed feeds back to HQ. What's more, the software-defined gateway SFPs can be repurposed to fulfill a range of different functions in the future.

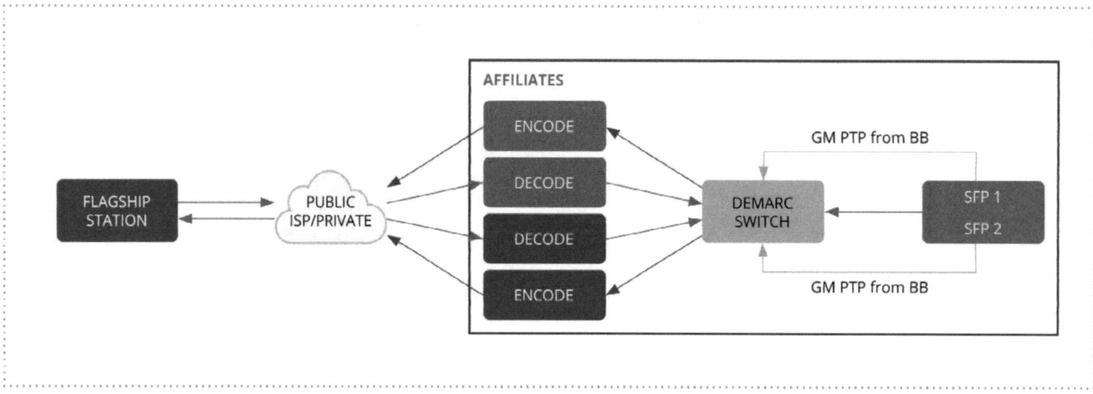


FIGURE 5. USE CASE OVERVIEW

The distribution part is rather straightforward, but things get a bit more complicated when it comes to synchronizing signals in this hybrid environment, as the decoders, encoders, and ST 2110 gateways need a PTP reference to be in sync. The answer to this problem was found in the Grand Master Add-On software, which enables the SFP processors to extract a sync reference from Black Burst/SDI signals. By installing this software in two or more gateway SFPs, the affiliate stations could also achieve redundancy of Grand Masters, fully synchronized to the VBI and compliant with ST 2059-2.

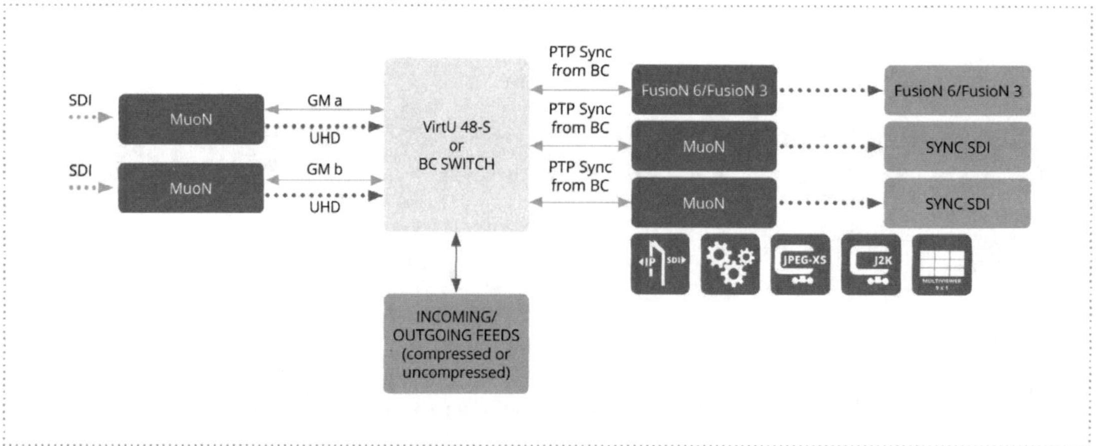


FIGURE 6. AFFILIATE STATION CONFIGURATION

## Processing SFP with Grand Master Functionality

The following image shows the PTP Grand Master functionality block inside the processing SFP. The Grand Master has no knowledge of the real Epoch time, but it can use the switch boundary Epoch time as a starting point to generate its internal time, therefore having slaves referencing their essences on a precise epoch time. The SFP can also be used to set the Epoch of the boundary clock by setting the Epoch on the Grand Master device once.

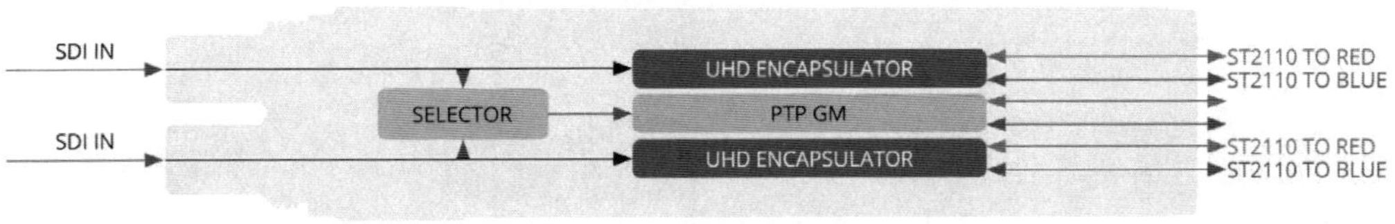


FIGURE 7. SFP DUAL ENCAPSULATOR WITH GRAND MASTER ADD-ON

## Demarcation Switch Configuration

Inside the demarcation switch, the SFPs generate the Grand Master clocks 1 and 2 for redundancy. Then the boundary clock does the Grand Master selection, and the reference of the system is set.

The Grand Master can receive the boundary clock synchronization signal on a different V-Lan, and can therefore use the Epoch time from the boundary clock. The slave's devices are synchronized with the boundary clock, which is a normal operation in IP switches equipped with boundary clock. At the same time, the MuoN B clocks are slave to the demarc switch on a virtual interface to sync their Epoch and are master to the demarc switch boundary clock on the secondary virtual interface.

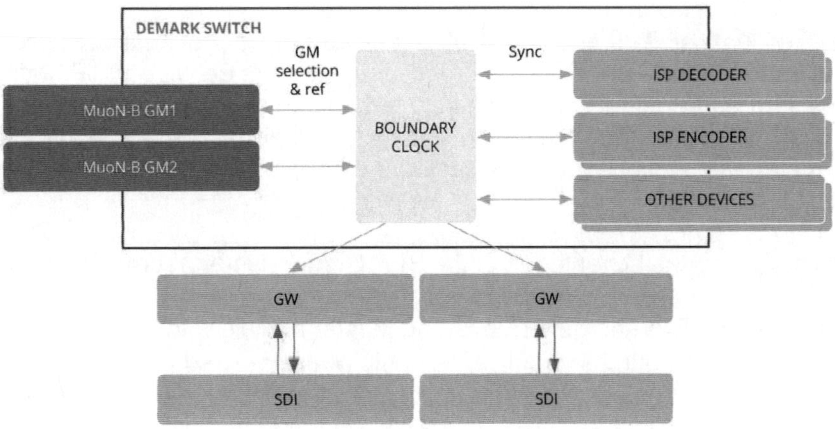


FIGURE 8. DEMARCATION SWITCH OVERVIEW

## Epoch

The Epoch in this use case is locally referenced and not synchronized to any GPS. Instead, the Epoch is manually set in the environment using the clock source with the most precise hold-over – the demarcation switch clock. It can either be forced via the switch CLI, or via the PTP BMCA algorithm. In the latter case, the Epoch is set on the SFP PTP Grand Master via its RESTful API.

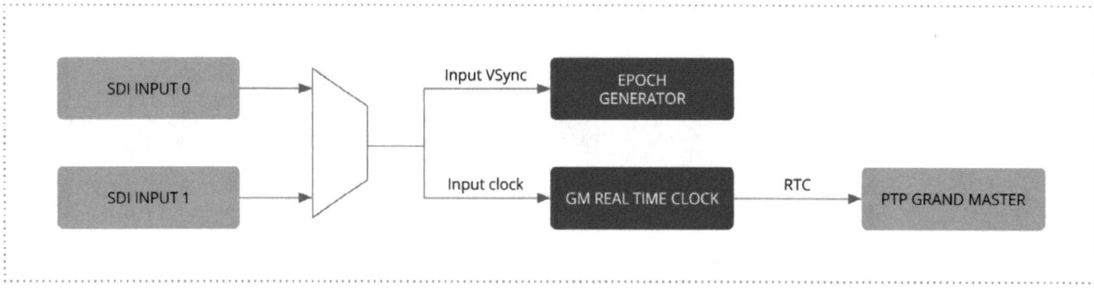


FIGURE 9. MUON B GRAND MASTER EPOCH FROM SWITCH BOUNDARY CLOCK

## Stability of the SFP Grand Master

During our work on the SFP Grand Master PTP generator, we observed that its stability is even better than that of a standard switch boundary clock in free-run mode. We also found that it is just as stable as a GPS-locked Grand Master signal due to the high refresh rate of the Grand Master in the SFP. The SFP Grand Master is updated and readjusted with every vertical sync, so the readjustments are done 60 times per second. The real time clock (RTC) of the SFP Grand Master Add-On is locked on the SPG SDI reference clock using the input recovered clock. This way, the RTC is always fully synchronized with the SPG, giving a highly precise clock. We observed a drift of one to three clock cycles (148Mhz clock) between the synchronized output from the de-encapsulator and the studio Black Burst.

## Conclusion

The Grand Master Add-On installed on ST2110/UHD gateway SFPs proved a viable solution to distribute and synchronize signals between the broadcast network's central, full-IP station and its remote SDI locations. Not only did this approach help reduce the affiliates' system complexity, but it also enabled the customer to minimize the cost of initiating its gradual move to IP. With the SFP solution installed, the affiliate stations are now ready to address ST 2110 feeds, taking them one step closer to becoming full-IP stations.

Let us conclude by reviewing the advantages of the SFP Grand Master approach for this specific use case:

- Ability to encapsulate SDI and generate Grand Master signals with a single device
- No extra hardware cost, purchase of licenses only where needed
- Easy integration, reduced cost and effort, uses already existing master sync reference
- As stable as (if not more stable than) a real PTP Grand Master

Besides the one presented in this paper, there are countless other applications for this SFP Grand Master solution. Other potential use cases include remote applications where GPS is not available and budgets are limited, or facilities that want to pursue a gradual migration of their legacy SDI systems to hybrid infrastructures. It might also be of value for proof-of-concept phases, as it enables broadcasters to test the ST 2110 equipment of various vendors without having to buy expensive SPGs.

# IP Network Operation Center (IP NOC): The Future for Broadcast

**Claudio Lisman**
**ProximaVision Corporation**
**Bal Harbour, Florida, United States**

**Abstract** – As IP continues to go mainstream for video production, producers have identified key requirements.They're looking to move away from bulky, expensive hardware to more flexible software and cloud-based solutions as well as more lightweight field gear like bonded cellular backpacks. IP streaming solutions need to be incorporated easily into production workflows, with the ability to ingest non-baseband sources. Broadcast operations need to be able to use the entire gamut of IP-based protocols,and sometimes several of them during the same production. Likewise, they need fast, frictionless ways to transcode feeds and files into multiple video house formats for asset management and distribution.

## From RF and Baseband to IP

The media industry's evolution from baseband to IP turned into a revolution in 2020. With the global pandemic shuttering studios, emptying broadcast operations centers and sidelining OB trucks, streaming and broadcast productions were forced to double down on remote production workflows and technologies. Consequently, they embraced IP like never before, together with its game-changing efficiency, cost savings and flexibility for meeting rapidly changing requirements.

As IP continues to go mainstream for video production, producers have identified key requirements. They're looking to move away from bulky, expensive hardware to more flexible software and cloud-basedsolutions as well as more lightweight field gear like bonded cellular backpacks.

They need IP streaming solutions that can be incorporated easily into production workflows, with the ability to ingest non-baseband sources. Broadcast operations need to be able to use the entire gamut of IP-based protocols, and sometimes several of them during the same production. Likewise, they need fast, frictionless ways to transcode feeds and files into multiple video house formats for asset management anddistribution.

The concept of an IP network operations center (IP NOC) addresses all of these requirements by bringing together the state of the art in IP-based signal acquisition and cloud-based media asset management (MAM). Driven by these enabling technologies, the IP NOC offers a paradigm shift from traditional broadcast operation centers and satellite trucks to smaller and more nimble transmission gear, cameras and capture devices.

IP-based systems offer the ability to acquire signals from a virtually unlimited number of inputs using a wide range of protocols (SRT, WebRTC, HLS, RTSP, etc.), then output via an ethernet switch for live multicamera monitoring, real-time transcoding to house formats, live editing, and finally publication, distribution, and/or re-transmission

### A Powerful Evolution and Building the Foundation to the IP NOC

Traditional broadcast systems using SDI require dedicated routing switchers, video monitors and ingest hardware. While they offer reliability and high quality, they are inflexible and limited in terms of the number of inputs and outputs that can be achieved without adding additional hardware routing switchers. Adding additional output formats for edit, MAM and playout are equally cumbersome.

In contrast, IP-based systems offer the ability to acquire signals from a virtually unlimited number of inputsusing a wide range of protocols (SRT, WebRTC, HLS, RTSP, etc.), then output via an Ethernet switch for live multicamera monitoring, real-time transcoding to house formats, live editing and finally publication, distribution and/or retransmission.

And there's good news for broadcasters who are taking a phased approach to the IP migration: With an IP-NOC topology, they don't need to drop SDI entirely—IP streaming, NDI and SDI can coexist in the same workflow.

The IP revolution is also having an impact on outside broadcasting and on-location newsgathering. Traditionally, remote broadcast teams have had to rely on OB trucks, large antennas, and plenty of logistical and technical wrangling just to get a signal back to the broadcast operation center. Today, bondedcellular transmission radically simplifies remote production and live contribution, replacing those unwieldy antennas and expensive uplink trucks with devices small enough to hold in your hand or, at most,wear in a backpack.

### From Today to Tomorrow

The paradigm shift from broadcast operations centers and satellite trucks to IP-based network operations centers and smaller and more nimble transmission gear, cameras, and capture devices was well underway before 2020, but the unprecedented events of this last years have forced production teams to make the leapnow.

The first key component in the IP NOC is advanced video production and distribution technology for remote video capture. For effective IP video streaming and broadcast, this component should include thefollowing attributes:

- Ability to capture content from any IP stream, camera or broadcast source, including SRT, NDI, HLS,RTSP, DASH and even SDI, taking incoming feeds from both baseband and non-baseband sources.
- Ability to transcode live content in real time into broadcast formats (ProRes, XDCAM, AVC-Intra, DVCPRO, H.264 and H.265/HEVC) for fast integration into production, management and deliveryworkflows.
- Ability to work with both HD and 4K UHD signals.
- Support for real-time editing in Apple Final Cut Pro X and Adobe Premiere Pro, enabling editors topreview and edit live streams in those NLEs while the video feed is still being captured.
- A software solution that manages all streams in real time without costly hardware decoders.

## Figures:

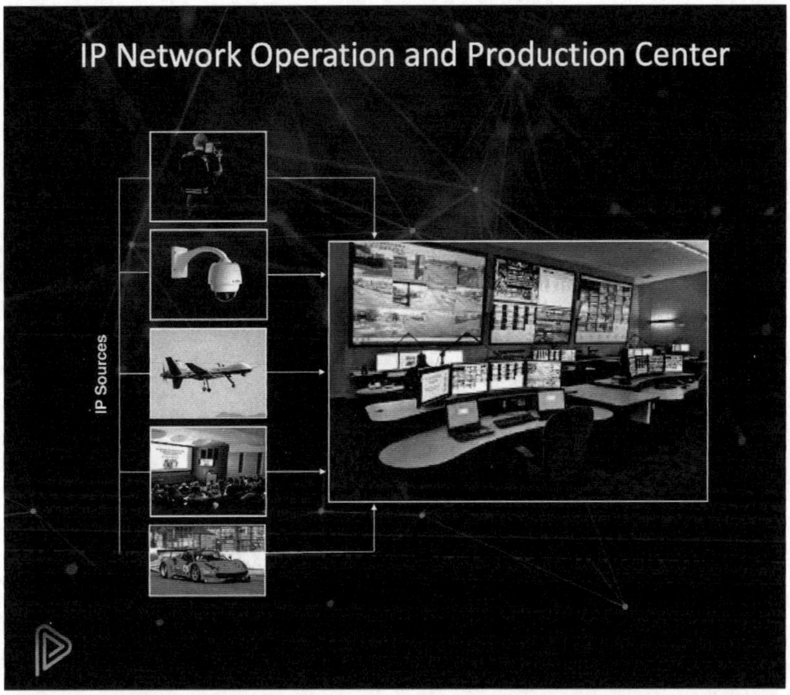


FIGURE 1: BROADCASTERS CAN ASSEMBLE AN ENTIRE IP OPERATION CENTER WITH OFF-THE-SHELF HARDWARE AND ACQUIRE SIGNALS FROM ALL MANNER OF IP SOURCES.

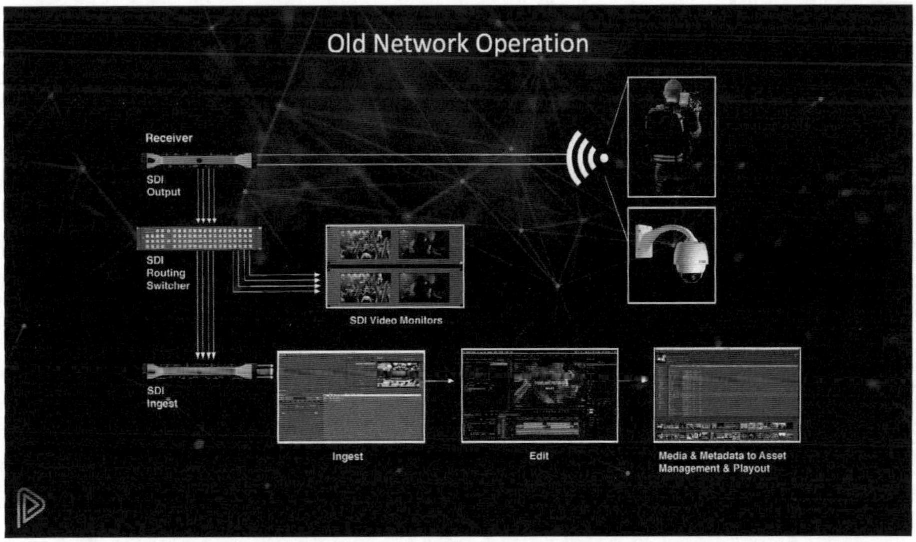


FIGURE 2: AN SDI-BASED WORKFLOW.

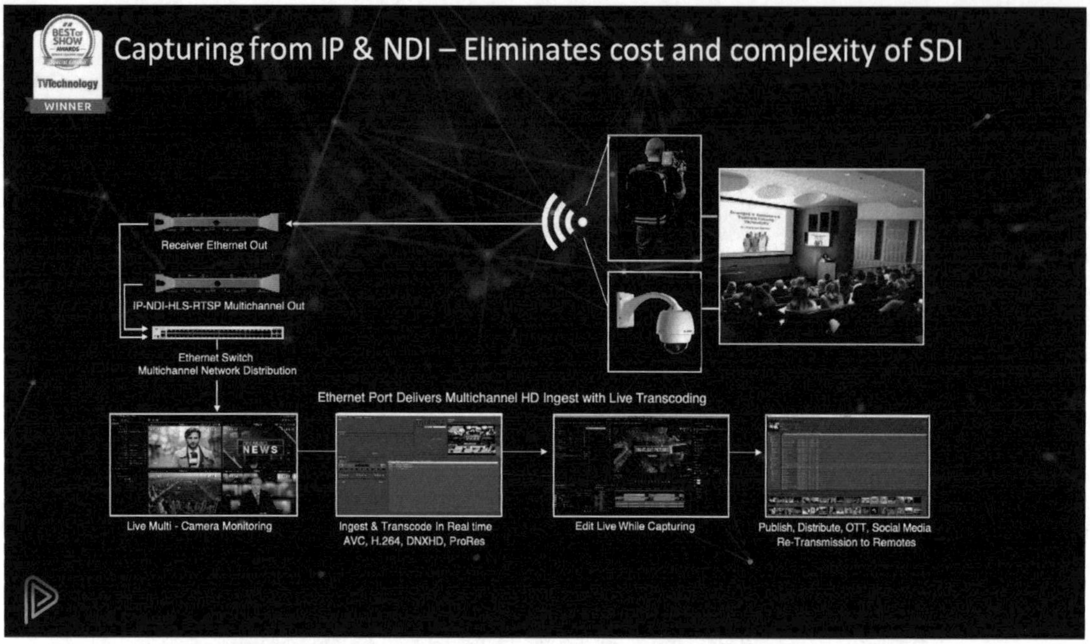


FIGURE 3. AN IP-BASED WORKFLOW AND NETWORK OPERATIONS CENTER.

# IPMX for Broadcast Installations

**Jean Lapierre, André Testa**
**Matrox Video**
**Montréal, Canada**
jlapierr@matrox.com, atesta@matrox.com

**Abstract** – The SMPTE ST 2110 open standard based protocol has seen massive adoption in the Broadcast industry in the recent years, as it offers a great migration path from SDI. Similarly, the Pro AV industry is also shifting its infrastructure toward AV over IP. However, the absence of standards-based protocols is causing the emergence of multiple proprietary solutions. IPMX (Internet Protocol Media Experience) was created with the intent to adapt the proven SMPTE ST 2110 suite of standards to the unique needs of the Pro AV markets, while ensuring that IPMX devices are interoperable with SMPTE ST 2110 devices. This interoperability is set to benefit the Broadcast industry as IPMX devices could help address particular use case issues currently affecting the industry.

## Introduction

The Pro AV's industry shift to AV over IP is now reality. But unlike the Broadcast industry, there are no true open standards for transporting and managing the Audio and Video signals in Pro AV. After successfully promoting and adopting the SMPTE ST 2110 suite of standards in the Broadcast industry, AIMS was tasked to so the same for the Pro AV market. The benefits of having standards-based protocols are undeniable as interoperable solutions have been a vital industry driver of growth and success for decades.

The SMPTE ST 2110 standard for transport and the AMWA NMOS specification for control cover the functionality required for a complete set of standards in Pro AV. A few areas, however, require some adaptation and modification to meet the needs of the Pro AV market. The idea is to leverage the work already undertaken and build on it by incorporating features specific to the Pro AV market. This is precisely the mission of IPMX.

## IPMX in a Nutshell

IPMX is based on the SMPTE ST 2110 suite of standards for transport protocols, which includes ST 2059 PTP for timing requirements and RTP based on the ST 2110 specifications. IPMX is also based on the AMWA NMOS specification for the control layer: IS-04 is used for registration and discovery, IS-05 for connection; IS-08 for audio channel mapping; as well as for security and best practices. IPMX builds on this foundation by incorporating features specific to the Pro AV market, including simplified timing, asynchronous sources support, HDCP support for protected content, compressed video, Forward error correction, and others which will be briefly covered next. These features are summarized in the JT-NM Pro AV Technology Roadmap [1]. The IPMX roadmap is divided in three phases (see Figure 1 for phase 1).

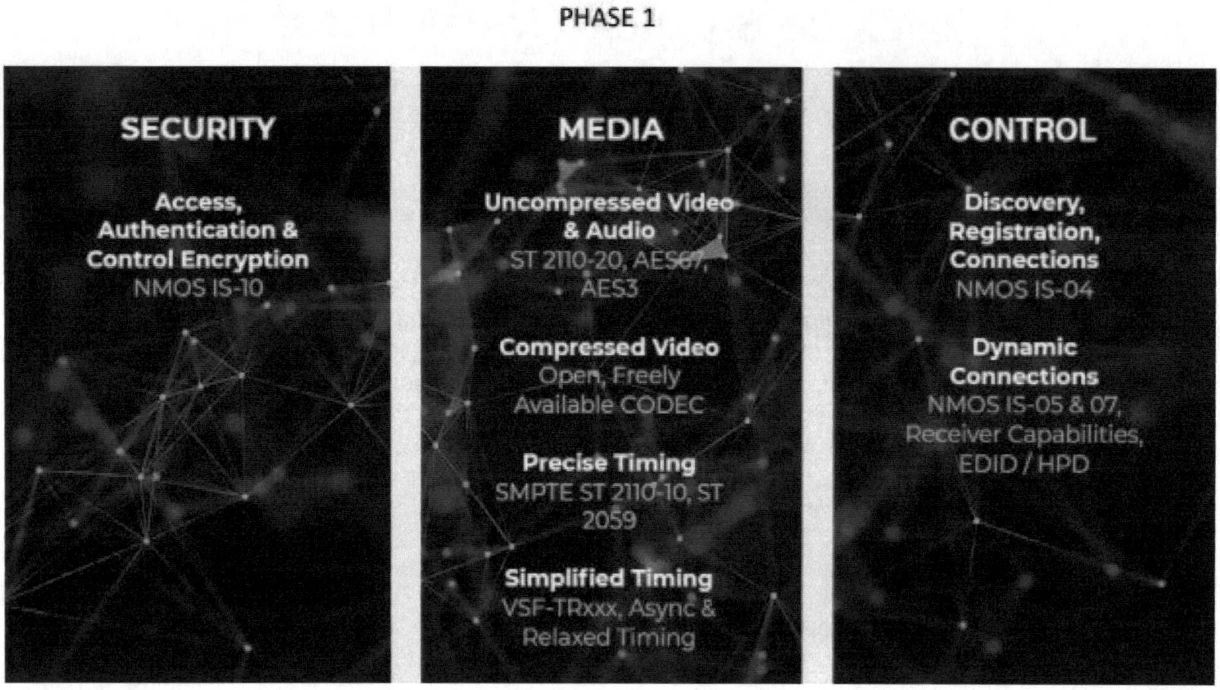


FIGURE 1: JT-NM PROAV TECHNOLOGY ROADMAP.

### PTP Support

The PTP profile and timing accuracy mandated by IPMX are designed to make it easier to implement a grandmaster. It eliminates the need to be locked to the SI second, or for traceability, and the frequency accuracy is expected to be better than 100 ppm. Moreover, the default IPMX profile generates 32 times less traffic than SMPTE ST 2110, resulting in fewer loads on the grandmaster and on the network. IPMX thus reduces the need for network equipment with special support for PTP. IPMX is also designed to support workflows where no PTP is available.

### Asynchronous Sources

SMPTE ST 2110 supports asynchronous sources, although these are not typical of ST 2110 installations. In IPMX, asynchronous sources are the norm, and supporting them efficiently was paramount. In Pro AV, it is crucial to support very low in-to-out latency. IPMX adds some controls to enable users to optimise the latency in their IPMX network by synchronizing the Playout time of all relevant devices to their minimum possible value.

### HDCP Support

HDCP is the copy protection scheme used to encrypt signals carried over HDMI and DisplayPort. Pro AV makes extensive use of devices with HDCP encrypted material. IPMX influenced the Direct Adaptation Amendment released recently by DCP [2]. This amendment defines the method for applying HDCP on an RTP stream (see Figure 2).

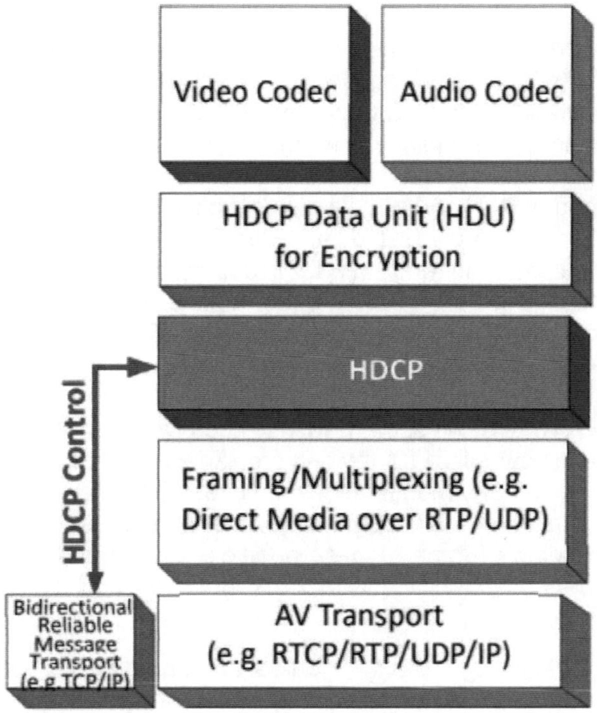


FIGURE 2: HDCP BLOCK DIAGRAM.

### Video Compression

Supporting existing infrastructure is critical in Pro AV. Support for Gigabit Ethernet network over existing Cat5e or Cat6 cables is imperative, for example, because we want to leverage these common and popular infrastructures. Most IPMX installations are expected to be compressed video installations. An ultra low latency codec with a high quality capable of sub 1 Gigabit transport of UHD video and computer graphics is also part of IPMX.

### Forward Error Correction

IPMX supports ST 2022-7 but its cost is often prohibitive. On the other hand, offering no packet protection is not desirable either. IPMX is therefore working to provide an improved Forward Error Correction technique that supports low latency, low overhead, and very high Time Before Failure.

## IPMX in ST 2110 Networks

In the last paragraphs we see how IPMX adds to SMPTE ST 2110. Let us now look at how these additions can be of interest to broadcasters, especially to those already deploying ST 2110 in their installations. One of the main drivers for ST 2110 and IPMX is to be able to use off-the-shelf IT infrastructure equipment instead of custom broadcast or custom Pro AV solutions. The goal is to benefit from the economy of scale and the added flexibility of IP networks. It should be noted that the Pro AV market is bigger than the Broadcast market. There exist far more Pro AV sites than Broadcast sites, and there are more Pro AV manufacturers to accommodate a wide range of equipment, prices, and functionality for this market. But just as the Broadcast industry moved to using less expensive HDMI monitors, so it is expected to start using IPMX. Broadcasters did not replace all their SDI monitors. We will see a similar situation develop with broadcasters using a mix of ST 2110 and IPMX devices, depending on the use case and the problems they are trying to solve.

## Interoperability

While developing IPMX we were regularly asked about the compatibility between IPMX and SMPTE ST 2110. Care must be taken to explain the relationship between the two because it is important to understand what IPMX can do and when it can be used with ST 2110 equipment. Hopefully this will make it easier to understand how IPMX devices can be used in a Broadcaster's ST 2110 network.

As we saw earlier, IPMX supports PTP and has its own simplified profile. But IPMX also mandates that the PTP profile used by ST 2110 be supported by all IPMX followers. This is a *shall* in the specification, meaning that an IPMX device can be added to a ST 2110 network that has an ST 2059-compliant grandmaster without any issues. Because IPMX is based on the ST 2110 RTP protocol, the IPMX network protocol is compatible with ST 2110 devices. So, when IPMX devices are in a ST 2110 network they can interoperate with ST 2110 devices.

IPMX is also based on AMWA NMOS. As such, IPMX devices can be discovered, and their signals routed and controlled the same way ST 2110 devices are. An existing broadcast controller can be used with IPMX devices without needing any modifications if it uses IS04 and IS-05. IPMX and ST 2110 devices can be mixed and matched in a ST 2110 environment. However, IPMX adds new capabilities to support additional Pro AV workflows. Some of these additions may impose limitations to the interaction between IPMX and ST 2110.

## ST 2110 Network

In a broadcast environment, everything is usually genlocked to a reference and all signals coming into a ST 2110 Sender are aligned with PTP, as shown in Figure 3.

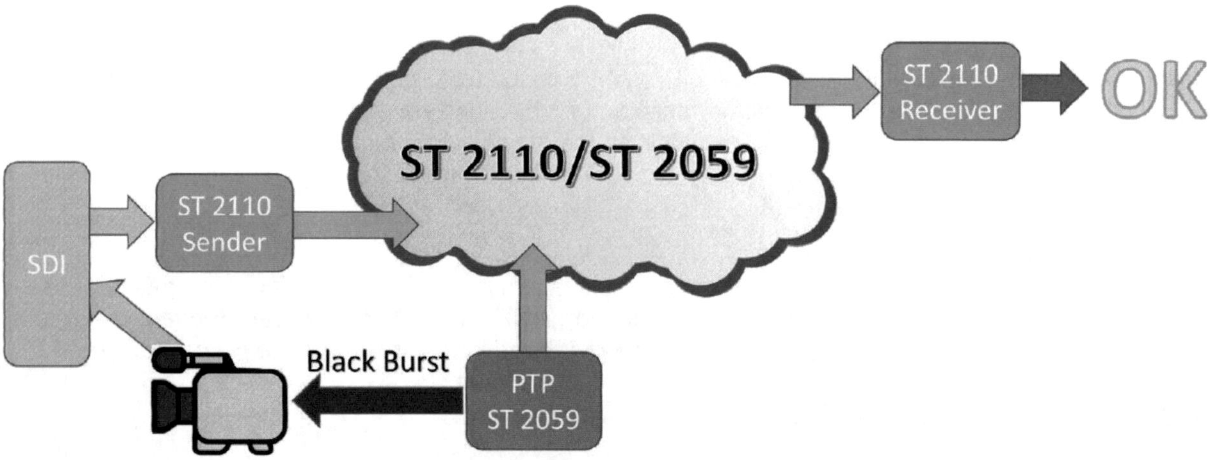


FIGURE 3: TYPICAL ST 2110 NETWORK.

As previously stated, since IPMX devices are compatible with an ST 2110 network containing an ST 2059 compliant grandmaster, everything will work as expected, as depicted in Figure 4. IPMX Senders will behave identically to ST 2110 Senders and consequently will be received by both the IPMX and ST 2110 Receivers. IPMX receivers are designed to also receive ST 2110-compliant signals.

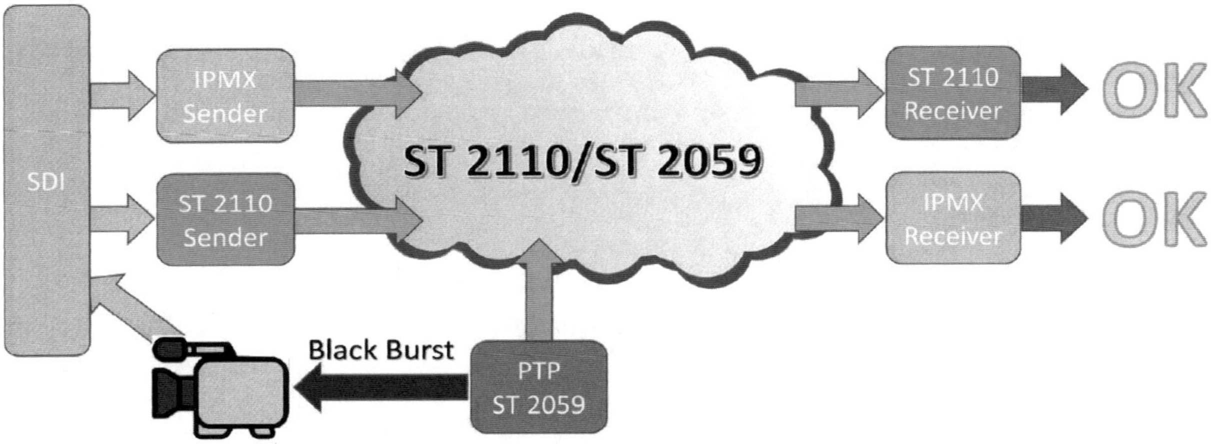


FIGURE 4: IPMX DEVICES INTEGRATED WITHIN A TYPICAL ST 2110 NETWORK.

## Asynchronous Signals

In Pro AV, sources are often asynchronous. The mandatory support of asynchronous sources is one of the main characteristics of IPMX. This represents a major difference with ST 2110 and, as such, support is optional. So, what happens when we add a source that is asynchronous to our network? Figure 5 illustrates the addition of a laptop with a DisplayPort output. Since this laptop is not compliant with any ST 2110 compatible genlock mechanism, the RTP stream generated by the IPMX Sender will not be locked to the SMPTE ST 2059 epoch as the other ST 2110 Senders in the network are.

FIGURE 5: ASYNCHRONOUS SOURCE IN ST 2110 NETWORK.

As per the IPMX specification, the IPMX receiver will reproduce the signal from the laptop as if it is connected directly to that monitor. The main goals of IPMX are no skipped frames, no repeated frames, and minimal latency. Some ST 2110 devices may successfully receive the signal, but the video viewed on the monitor will depend on the implementation. On a Software Multiviewer the result might look like any other ST 2110 source. Other devices might apply some kind of time-base correction (TBC) to the signal. And some might look at the SDP file, see that it is not a synchronous signal, and refuse to connect because they are not designed to support that use case. It must be understood that if we use a ST 2110 Sender that supports asynchronous signals as described in the ST 2110 specification, a signal very similar to the one from the IPMX Sender would be generated. The results at the output of that ST 2110 Receiver would be the same as for the IPMX Sender.

### Content Protection

Support for HDCP sources is important in Pro AV. HDCP is not part of any ST 2110 specs, so if using an HDCP encrypted media source for the IPMX Sender, the ST 2110 Receiver will not receive that signal. IPMX Receivers that support HDCP can be expected to reproduce the signal without an issue. There are some use cases where an IPMX Sender will produce a signal that a ST 2110 Receiver will not be able to properly receive.

### IPMX versus ST 2110

In summary, how do IPMX and ST 2110 interoperate?

- IPMX Senders and Receivers can fully operate within ST 2110 networks
- IPMX Receivers can successfully receive signals from ST 2110 Senders
- ST 2110 Receivers
  - can successfully receive IPMX signals from synchronous sources
  - might successfully receive IPMX signals from asynchronous sources
  - will not successfully receive IPMX signals that are HDCP protected

## Using IPMX in a Broadcast Environment

The differences and particularities between IPMX and SMPTE ST 2110 have been explained. We can now identify where and how broadcasters might benefit from IPMX in their installations.

### HDMI and DisplayPort

IPMX mainly targets media sources like computers, set-top boxes, and other devices that use HDMI and DisplayPort interfaces. If transmitting and receiving these types of signals is required, IPMX might be a good solution. Finding an ST 2110 device that includes such support might not be trivial, but this support comes natively in IPMX. However, special care must be taken in adding IPMX to the current workflow. Figure 6 depicts a scenario where a DisplayPort signal is introduced to an ST 2110 network using an IPMX Sender. If that signal is to be used with a ST 2110 device, then care must be taken to make sure the device supports asynchronous signals. In the case of an IPMX Receiver that drives a DisplayPort monitor, this will always work no matter if the source is ST 2110 or IPMX. It provides a good example of a simple use of IPMX in a broadcast setting.

FIGURE 6: DISPLAYPORT SOURCE IN ST 2110 NETWORK.

### Set-top Boxes

Broadcasters sometimes need to use set-top boxes to monitor TV signals. With IPMX devices, the ST 2110 network can be used to distribute these signals anywhere within a facility. This will invariably require the use of HDCP-enabled devices on both ends, as shown in Figure 7. The IPMX Sender that supports HDCP transmits a protected signal in the network and the IPMX Receivers that also include HDCP support can successfully receive that signal and retransmit it to the HDMI monitor.

FIGURE 7: ADDING A SET-TOP BOX TO A NETWORK AND DISTRIBUTING ITS FEED ACROSS THE FACILITY.

## New Multiviewer Capability

HDCP support is built into IPMX, but it is not specific to IPMX, meaning that the HDCP Direct adaptation amendment [2] is a method to support HDCP on any RTP signal.

Multiviewers often use HDMI monitors that support HDCP. It is technically possible for a multiviewer manufacturer to add support for HDCP to their device, the same way an IPMX device can add support for HDCP. This adds a new workflow capability for broadcasters by having an HDCP-enabled multiviewer to monitor set-top box signals the same way it does for non-HDCP enabled signals on the network.

FIGURE 8: HDCP-ENABLED MULTIVIEWER.

## Television Studio Video Wall

Video walls are common in Pro AV, but they are also widely used in Broadcast. With IPMX, broadcasters can simply connect next-generation IPMX video walls to their ST 2110 network. Note that IPMX video walls will be able to display and mix content from both IPMX and ST 2110 sources. It would even be possible to make sure all the monitors are locked to the house sync through PTP, if there is a need for such a configuration.

## KVM

IPMX has a lot to offer to IP KVM devices. Broadcasters have adopted KVM, but a KVM that is compatible with SMPTE 2110 would be compelling since it could share the same network infrastructure. This would make it easier to deploy new AV-over-IP workflows because of IPMX and ST 2110. The audio and video signals produced by a KVM device can be used as any audio and video signals. This could be used in scenarios such as training, reviewing, directing, among others. KVM signals could easily be monitored by a multiviewer, so many new workflows could be enabled with this capability.

## Expanding Monitoring Capability

Increased compression ratio targeted by IPMX can provide new opportunities. As mentioned earlier, support for existing Gigabit Ethernet is paramount; IPMX is therefore targeting 800 Mbit/s bandwidth for Ultra HD Video signals or 200 Mbit/s for HD Video signals. These are much lower than the usual Broadcast compression ratios. This opens up the possibility to monitor AV signals using a laptop, for example. Figure 9 demonstrates the case where the output of a multiviewer is fed to an IPMX Sender, which in turn compresses the signal to a bandwidth small enough that it can be received by a laptop instead of using a ST 2110 converter to HDMI. Moreover, software on the laptop can be added to monitor and analyze incoming signals.

FIGURE 9: USING LAPTOP TO PERFORM MONITORING TASKS.

## Conclusion

This paper aims to clarify the similarities and differences between IPMX and SMPTE ST 2110 so that broadcasters see the benefit of adding IPMX devices within their ST 2110 network to solve specific problems. More specifically, IPMX devices can be added and used in existing broadcast ST 2110 networks. IPMX devices are discovered, managed, and routed the same way ST 2110 equipment is, with no specific requirement for a separate controller. IPMX Receivers can successfully receive ST 2110 signals, but there are some cases where ST 2110 Receivers might not successfully receive IPMX signals. Our goal is to demonstrate that IPMX can be another useful tool in addressing broadcast problems. IPMX introduces technology can be added to broadcast equipment, providing new capabilities that might even enable completely new workflows within the broadcast industry.

## References

[1] https://static.jt-nm.org/documents/jt-nm_proav-technology-roadmap-v1.0.pdf

[2] https://www.digital-cp.com/sites/default/files/HDCP%20Direct%20Adaptation%20Amendment%20Spec%20Rev2_3.pdf

# NDI In the Master Control Room

**Fabio Gattari**
**Etere Pte Ltd, Singapore**
**Singapore**
marketing@etere.com

**Abstract** –It's no secret that NDI is the new face of revolution in information transmitting. Capable of higher quality information transfer, broadcast quality videos can be delivered and received in a frame-accurate format. This high-quality transmission makes it an ideal choice for switching in a live production environment within the Master Control room. NDI streams are able to transmit a full frame full resolution version of videos and a lower resolution proxy version that can reduce the load on networks when streaming to multi-viewers, vision mixers and preview screens. Its ability to multicast and switch to full resolution version of video transmissions makes it the ideal choice to use in a Master Control room.

## Introduction

This paper discusses the characteristics of NDI, its advantages in a master control room, its respective challenges and how to overcome the challenges effectively. In the included case study, we will explore how Mondo TV in Belgrade, Serbia, integrates NDI technology in the master control room effectively, making it the world's first fully NDI-connected system. The station, which went live on 28 June 2020, manages 40 playout channels using NDI technology and Etere Ecosystem software. In addition, the station also runs a live internet TV on Mondo TV's online platform as well as on Telecom Serbia's website for the local market.

### NDI Compatibility in the Master Control Room

NDI is known for its reliability. NewTek claims that NDI is an efficient, long-distance transmission capable of simultaneously sending high-quality, low-latency videos to multiple sources. NDI enables video and audio sources to be shared bi-directionally across a standard Ethernet local area network, eliminating the need for direct connections, costly cable runs and infrastructure upgrades. Furthermore, Newtek NDI is available royalty free for both developers and users.

These characteristics make NDI the perfect choice for use in broadcasting, its long reach and stability an improvement from the hassle and unreliability of SDI connections. In fact, NDI is already being incorporated into many broadcasting companies around the world. However, SDI being a long-standing information transfer technology is not without its own merits. In this paper, we will explore the extent of NDI's advantages in the Master Control room, its respective challenges and how to overcome them.
In terms of usage in the Master Control room and in fast paced environments, NDI has a few main advantages, namely its flexibility in creating new linkages quickly and its cost-efficiency qualities.

This paper is excerpted from the Proceedings of the 2021 NAB Broadcast Engineering and Information Technology (BEIT) Conference, © 2021, National Association of Broadcasters, 1 M Street S.E., Washington, DC 20003 USA.

## Broadcast Potential of NDI

The broadcast potential of an IP protocol is the most important aspect when considering usage in the Master Control room. As such, one of NDI's biggest advantages is its ability to run multiple streams simultaneously at no additional cost.

A user can send a large video file to the mixer with low latency, while at the same time, stream it as well as capture it on another network, making it not only flexible, but very useful in a fast-paced environment such as in the Master Control room. NDI is a bi-directional protocol that supports multiple streams of video simultaneously. It supports all resolutions, frame rates and video streams.

Additionally, any generation of NDI is able to work seamlessly with other generations as NDI is backwards compatible in software. Although NDI's high powered, flexible stream format is what makes the stream so well known, it can also be a hindrance in terms of usage in the Master Control room. The NDI stream does not come equipped with a fixed name, thus creating a disparity in its usage in the Master Control room.

As the master control requires a fixed connection, the NDI protocol cannot be used without additional help. Each signal used must be equipped with a unique identifier in the NDI name. This step takes great importance when linking the signals correctly, for example, two studio signals can be named "Studio 1" and "Studio 2". This step is important, and it requires prior planning, especially when the source signals start to number in the hundreds.

To ensure a continued stable connection, the dynamic list of sources must be periodically checked for conflicts. There is also the issue of the burden on the server, as NDI takes up a bandwidth that increases with the size of the audience. For example, a HD stream may consume up to 200MB, and that number will increase to 800MB if 4 listeners tune in. But this hiccup is not without a remedy. An NDI stream can be kept usable when it is applied with strategic planning in place. The bandwidth needs to be used with proper planning to avoid unnecessary streams and to effectively allocate streaming servers to distribute videos to many locations, similar to SDI distributors.

To eliminate the challenge of manual switching in transmission, the integration of Dynamic Host Configuration Protocol (DHCP) enables an automated and dynamic assignment of IP parameters, IP address, network mask, switch address and name server addressed to each PC/server on the LAN network. In addition, DHCP also automates the assignment of network-parameters to the related network devices.

As a result of the integration, the manual tasks of creating and maintaining of IP address assignments for each client/server is eliminated. The integration of DHCP in Etere IP transmission provides a centralized, server-based setup that reduces the manual tasks of creation and maintenance of IP address assignments for each client/server; the centralized database pools resources for effective optimization and eliminates duplicate resource assignments. Moreover, DHCP allows operators to automatically upgrade the software on client systems.

### Ease of Incorporation in Master Control Room

But is NDI feasible to be used in the Master Control room in terms of its ease of incorporation? The nature of NDI's cost-saving and flexible qualities can make the transition from SDI systems to NDI achievable. The move from SDI to a new IP protocol can commonly be seen as a costly change, but with NDI, users are able to use low-cost converters to port over SDI signals to NDI.

NDI is capable of working in tandem with SDI, so the user is able to incorporate NDI for an initial network that links to an SDI endpoint, and switch completely to an NDI endpoint when budget becomes available. However, an issue with NDI would be that the NDI stream by itself requires additional software to utilize it to its full potential. For example, the necessity of audio and video monitoring requires an add-on software to be used in the workflow.

With NDI, the signals are not linear, so it can be seen as simple to monitor, but to be truly efficient the user needs to have an intelligent software to avoid unnecessary bandwidth use. Fortunately, NDI's popularity has continued to extend its support for many software applications in the market today. Popular software programs such as Skype, EasyWorship, and many others offer native NDI support. The requirement to employ additional software programs to use NDI can be seen as an unnecessary expense, but the nature of the software usage is kept scalable, meaning that there is no additional cost to expand the NDI powered systems, unlike with SDI, where the use of hardware increases the expense whenever there are system changes.

NDI's popularity in the software field has ensured that it has many compatible hardware such as NDI-enabled cameras from notable companies such as Panasonic, to optimize the Master Control room usage. NDI connects a wide variety of video devices including cameras, converters, video mixers, graphics systems and many other production devices.

Even if the user's initial systems are not compatible with NDI, with the use of an NDI convertor, NDI can be incorporated into the Master Control room. Without expensive high-speed network infrastructures or a major overhaul of existing infrastructure, broadcasters can transition to a versatile IP video facility easily with an NDI setup.

## Usage in Master Control Room

For usage in a Master Control room, another important factor to consider is the ability to preview streams before the content goes on air. Usually in an SDI-connected environment, the user will be able to fulfil this with a flip of a switch, but with NDI, a user requires sufficient connection time to do the same. This can be offset by using a system that makes use of a pre-set/program architecture, so that the switch can operate without any glitches. To connect with all NDI signals is not a correct option, because the system can have hundreds of NDI signals and connecting to them all could use up all your bandwidth. Thus, an intelligent pre-set must be used to be sure that the next source is always ready.

## Cost Saving Quality of NDI

Cost efficiency is one of NDI's biggest advantages. Let us explore the importance of NDI in the master control room and exactly how cost-efficient it is. The broadcast industry is fast-evolving and fast-paced. As the demand for better quality broadcast increases, the need for more adaptable technological tools increases.

There is increasing demand for both broadcasters and production companies to produce and transmit higher frame rates, leading to higher costs. But with the use of NDI, video feeds can be transmitted with high quality and low latency, at a much lower cost than a conventional SDI setup. In addition, NDI's ability to link multiple inputs is crucial when operating multiple cameras from the Master Control Room. In contrast, an SDI setup does not allow devices that are connected on a network to communicate with one another.

In addition, by using NDI enabled IP workflows, broadcasters can leverage the benefits of a streamlined IT and IP configuration process for a more cohesive network infrastructure. Newtek also states that NDI is the first ever codec to provide multi-generational stability as once a video signal is compressed, there is no quality loss.

All in all, transitioning to IP does not have to result in higher costs. In fact, moving to IP can be a long-term investment in cost-savings. For one, NDI allows businesses to respond quickly to changes. Unlike NDI, there are limitations in delivering content in more conventional ways such as an SDI setup. For example, the higher costs of scaling can restrict the flexibility and adaptability of the company.

On the contrary, using NDI allows broadcasters to add or manage more content across new media platforms easily. Furthermore, by eliminating the need to invest in new high-speed network infrastructure, costs are kept down while efficiency is maximized. NDI's performance over a GigE network makes it possible for broadcasters to tap on their existing infrastructure using SDI equipment. NDI setup provides the broadcaster with a stable connectivity for users to transmit high quality videos across IP networks in real-time with little to no delay. This provides broadcasters with maximum flexibility and cost-efficiency when moving from a conventional SDI setup to an NDI workflow.

## Case Study: Mondo TV Usage of NDI

FIGURE 1: MONDO TV SETUP

One prominent example of live NDI usage would be the Mondo TV systems. A large-scale broadcaster in Belgrade, Serbia, Mondo TV needed to manage 40 playout channels along with 3 recording studios and control rooms, an ingest facility and incoming feeds, plus audio dubbing facilities. During the project initialization phase, Mondo TV decided that an NDI system was the most ideal fit for their business objectives. One of the reasons is that NDI architecture features one to multiple outputs. This allows all the departments at Mondo TV to use a common NDI signal.

The system has been designed without the use of any SDI cables. Etere has outfitted their systems with NDI technology to connect all their software, hardware, and channels together, all without any SDI. Mondo TV is currently one of the world's largest solely NDI-powered broadcasting systems. Mondo TV incorporates Etere's integrated end-to-end management software across their software-defined newsroom, transcoding, playout, monitoring, air sales and scheduling modules, allowing them to manage their workflows from a centralized database with complete connectivity across the whole facility.

The system connects three production studios, each equipped with multiple robotic camera rigs, three studio control rooms, and three audio dubbing rooms. Each of the functions within the various rooms can be remotely controlled through the master control rooms. The wide array of outputs is kept well optimized and cost-friendly through the use of NDI, which ensures that the Mondo TV connections are constantly stable and fast, even while keeping the overhead costs low.

However, the multiple output sources means that the prearranged 1GB bandwidth reaches its maximum capacity easily. This high bandwidth makes the use of low resolutions options unnecessary. Mondo TV needs to manage their sources and destinations minutely to ensure that their operations run smoothly at all times.

As sending and receiving video streams across an IP network requires applications supporting video to be able to discover the receiving applications that are searching for video, the linkages of the NDI are one of the biggest challenges faced by Mondo TV when switching to a fully NDI-based system. Additionally, Mondo TV needed to synchronize all the signals in the system to professional broadcasting standards.

To ensure a seamless connectivity, Mondo TV needed to plan their NDI synchronization before their installation could even begin. The NDI connectivity needed to be sustainable, flexible, and fully realized to ensure no errors when broadcasting began. VPK, as the chief systems designer for Mondo TV, conducted thorough research to come up with the correct IP design that takes into account the direct and reverse DNS that is hugely beneficial to the NDI discovery and planning. The large number of channels, and fully automated systems amounts to over 150 sole NDI sources that Mondo TV needed to manage. VPK needed to design an appropriate system for a sustainable and easy discovery that would be able to display over 150 NDI sources.

Mondo TV overcomes these challenges with the use of an IP multicast system to create an environment for the discovery of NDI applications, all without any configuration needed. When using IP multicast, the multicast is seen by all the NDI receiving machines on the subnet. Source sends a single copy of data to a single multicast address which is then distributed to an entire group of recipients. This is able to distribute the NDI streams with minimum overload, thus ensuring that the broadcasts run smoothly without any risk of a crash. This method also helps to keep the costs low for Mondo TV, allowing them to reach a much wider audience without too much strain on their finances.

In addition, selecting the network location is an important criterion for the successful discovery and registration of NDI. For example, the domain network location is used for domain networks, such as those at enterprise workplaces. They are typically controlled by the network administrator and changes are usually not allowed. In such instances, the multicast DNS should be allowed at the domain level.

Driven by NDI technology, Mondo TV can stream from satellites, camera feeds, playout devices, local/remote sources and monitor all their feeds on a single dashboard.

Furthermore, being able to integrate into a centrally managed ecosystem allows a TV station to drive workflows across the facility and deliver efficiencies across the capture, production, management and delivery process.

Mondo TV has successfully implemented the world's first fully NDI connected system with a stable connectivity throughout the facility and minimal hardware requirements. It allows the station to do away with the usual master switcher panels, instead requiring only a software to manage their broadcast.

This allows the company to streamline its workflows and deliver content to market quickly, leading to greater productivity and efficiency.

With the flexibility of NDI, Mondo TV is able to able to fully adapt its environment into a fully IP master control system with precise timing, seamless routing and monitoring. Moreover, the solution does not require any other IP protocols, allowing the station to enjoy greater cost savings while not compromising on the reliability of the broadcast performance.

## References


[1] *"NDI Benefits"*, NewTek Knowledge Base https://support.newtek.com/hc/en-us/articles/115001950714-NDI-BENEFITS

[2] Sunter, Liz. "Everything you need to know about NDI." Jigsaw24, 19 September 2018, www.jigsaw24.com/articles/everything-you-need-to-know-about-ndi

[3] Perez, Ann. *"NDI® and NDI|HX for network video production."* Epiphan Video, 4 April 2019, www.epiphan.com/blog/ndi-ndihx-network-video-production/

[4] Baker, Chuck. "Magewell Adds Cost-Saving Encode-Only HDMI- and SDI-to-NDI® Converters." NewTek Studio, 9 May 2019, www.newtek.com/blog/magewell-adds-cost-saving-encode-only-hdmi-and-sdi-to-ndi-converters/

[5] Kota, Sanjeev. *"Broadcasting Industry Embraces NDI Protocol (While SDI Becomes Archaism)."* Chetu, www.chetu.com/blogs/media-and-broadcasting/broadcasting-industry-embraces-ndi.php

[6] Caliborne, Vickie. *"Video Over IP: Is NDI the Solution?"* PLSN, 4 June 2018, plsn.com/articles/video-digerati/video-over-ip-is-ndi-the-solution/

[7] "NDI Discovery and Registration" NewTek Knowledge Base https://support.newtek.com/hc/en-us/articles/218109477-NDI-Discovery-and-Registration

# AUTHOR INDEX